THE TLINGIT
An introduction to their culture and history

3rd Edition

by

Wallace M. Olson

HERITAGE RESEARCH
Box 210961, Auke Bay, Alaska, 99821
Ph. 907-789-3311   Fax. 907-789-3434

1997

Product of Alaska, USA
Written, typeset, printed entirely in Alaska.

Library of Congress Catalog Card Number 97-73617
The Tlingit: An introduction to their culture and history/
Wallace M. Olson

ISBN 0-9659009-0-8

PHOTO FRONT COVER: L. Vanessa George, whose Tlingit name is
Heex.ei, wears a head dress with the Beaver Crest of her family, the
Dei Shu Hit Taan, at Celebration '94. She represents the young
generation of Tlingit who proudly retain their ancient cultural traditions.
(Photo courtesy of Mark Kelley, Photographer, Juneau)

PHOTO BACK COVER: Participants at Celebration '94 ,wearing a
variety of ceremonial regalia, raise their voices in song. (Photo courtesy
of Mark Kelley, Photographer, Juneau.)

PREFACE

Over the years, many outstanding anthropologists and historians such as John Swanton, Frederica de Laguna, Ronald Olson, Kalvero Oberg and Catherine McClellan have provided a great deal of reliable information regarding Tlingit culture and history. In more recent times younger writers such as Sergei Kan, Nora and Richard Dauenhauer and Aldona Jonaitis, have carried on this scholarly tradition. More importantly, there are the Tlingit elders and historians who have provided the fundamental information upon which so many scholars have built. With improved technology such as audio and video recording, we have been able to capture a small amount of their wisdom and knowledge before it is lost.

What I have attempted to do here is to condense and distill as much of this information as I can. While part of it has been the result of my own research, a great deal of the information comes from the literature already written about the Tlingit. Some of it comes from my Tlingit friends who have been willing to share their information with me. Although much of the information comes from others, any mistakes or errors are my own.

I decided early on that I would not use footnotes. If I were to reference each fact or bit of data, the footnotes would be as long as the text. In place of footnotes, I will provide a select list of recommended readings at the end.

Although in this third edition I have tried to include the latest information based on documentary research and archaeological finds, it seems that each year there are new discoveries and so a few pieces of information may already be out of date. In spite of this shortcoming, the basic description has been warmly received by readers, university teachers and most of all by many Tlingit, and so

I have kept this new edition basically the same as the original, with only minor changes.

Finally, this is only meant to be an introduction to the Tlingit and their culture; it does not pretend to be a complete description. As an introduction, I hope that it will stimulate readers to expand their knowledge of this great cultural heritage. There may be some--Tlingit, anthropologists or academicians--who may not agree with what I say. I am willing to change any portions which are erroneous.

I want to thank Dr. Arthur Petersen for his assistance on the original manuscript, Legia Pate for proofreading and correcting my final drafts, Richard and Nora Dauenhauer and Jeff Leer for help in transcribing Tlingit. For this third edition, Steve Henrickson, Curator of Collections at the Alaska State Museum, has been very helpful in locating photographs and providing valuable information on artifacts. One of Juneau's foremost photographers, Mark Kelley, was most generous with his time, and has allowed me to use two of his photos on the cover of this book.

I owe a great deal to the many academics with whom I have worked and studied. But I owe even more to the many Tlingit who taught me so much about their culture and history. Of the Tlingit who have helped me, three of them have been most influential: my wife, Marie, her brother, William Dick; my wife's clan brother and my close friend, Walter Williams. To all of these contributors, I can only say "Gunalcheesh. Ho Ho."

Wallace M. Olson

MAP OF SOUTHEASTERN ALASKA
SHOWING TLINGIT K̲WAANS AREAS

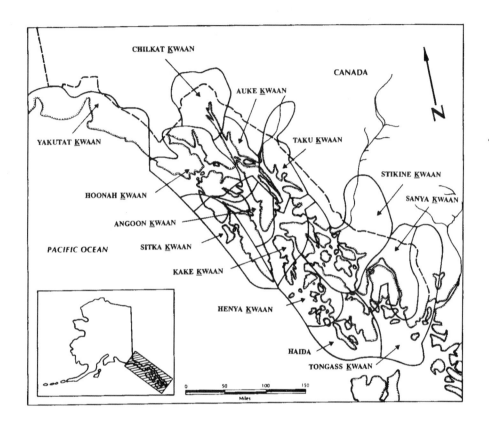

CHILKAT K̲WAAN

CANADA

AUKE K̲WAAN

YAKUTAT K̲WAAN

TAKU K̲WAAN

STIKINE K̲WAAN

HOONAH K̲WAAN

SANYA K̲WAAN

ANGOON K̲WAAN

PACIFIC OCEAN   SITKA K̲WAAN

KAKE K̲WAAN

HENYA K̲WAAN

HAIDA

TONGASS K̲WAAN

0   50   100   150

Miles

Adapted from: *Alaska's Heritage* by Joan M. Antonson and William S. Hanable
(Anchorage, Alaska Historical Commission, 1986, page 53)

i

KEY TO THE MAP

Traditional Name	Modern Name	Modern Settlements Settlements	Village Corporations
Yaakwdáat ḵwáan Gunaaxoo ḵwáan (a) Galyax ḵwáan (a)	Yakutat	Yakutat	Yak-tat ḵwáan
Jilḵaat ḵwáan Lḵoot ḵwáan(a)	Chilkat	Klukwan, Haines, Skagway	Klukwan Inc. Klukwan Corp (b)
Xunáa ḵaawu Aak'w ḵwáan	Hoonah, Auke	Hoonah, Gustavus, Elfin Cove Juneau, (Auke Bay)	Huna Totem Goldbelt
T'aaḵu ḵwáan S'awdaan ḵwáan (a)	Taku	Juneau (Douglas)	Goldbelt
Xutsnoowú ḵwáan	Angoon	Angoon, Tenakee Springs (c)	Kootznoowoo
Sheet'ká ḵwáan	Sitka	Sitka, Pelican	Shee Atika
Ḵéix' ḵwáan	Kake	Kake, Port Alexander	Kake Tribal
Shtax'heen ḵwáan	Stikine	Wramgell, Petersburg, Meyers Chuck,, Thorne Bay Coffman Cove (d)	
Heinyaa ḵwáan Henya (Lawaak ḵwáan) Kuyu ḵwáan (a)		Klawock, Point Baker, Port Protection	Klawock Heenya

ii

Saanyaa kwáan	Sanya	Saxman	Cape Fox

Taant'a kwáan   Tongass   Ketchikan, Metlakatla (e)
(T'angass kwáan)

HAIDA TERRITORY   Craig, Hollis, Hydaburg,   Hydaburg
Deeikeenaa ("Far Out")
Kasaan   Kavilco, Inc.

INLAND TLINGIT, CANADA
Aa Tlein Kwáan   Atlin   British Columbia
Tas Tlein Kwáan   Teslin   Yukon Territory

(a) Former kwáans, no longer distinguished as separate.

(b) This is a village corporation formed under the Indian Reorganization Act, 1934.

(c) Originally part of Xutsnoowú kwáan, Tenakee Inlet was given to the Wooshkeetaan clan.

(d) No village corporations because of stipulations in ANCSA. These "landless" Natives are now seeking land and compensation.

(e) Metlakatla is a Tsimshian Indian Reservation.

CONTENTS

PHOTOS

FIGURE

ORIGIN OF THE COUNTRY

This man was named Petrel and lived by the Nass River. Raven wanted this water because there was none to drink in this world, but Petrel always slept by his spring, and he had a cover over it so as to keep it all to himself. Then Raven came in and said to him, "My brother-in-law, I have just come to see you. How are you?" He told Petrel of all the things that were happening outside, to get him to go out to look at them.

But Petrel was too smart to fall for that trick and refused to go outside. When night came, Raven said, "I am going to sleep with you, brother-in-law." So they went to bed, and towards morning Raven heard Petrel sleeping very soundly. Then he quietly went outside to get some dog manure to put around Petrel's buttocks. When the dawn came, Raven said, "Wake up, wake up, brother-in-law, you have messed all over your clothes." So Petrel got up, and seeing that it was true, took his blankets and went outside. Raven rushed over to Petrel's spring, took off the cover, and began drinking. After he had drunk almost all of the water, Petrel came in and saw him. Then Raven flew straight up, crying "Gaa"....

Raven journeyed farther north. First he let some water fall from his mouth and made the Nass River. By and by he spit out more water and made the Stikine River. Next he spit out the Taku River, then the Chilkat, then the Alsek, and all the other large rivers. The small drops that came out of his mouth created the small salmon creeks. Then Raven went on again and came to a large town where there were people who had never seen daylight. They were out catching candlefish [Eulachon] in the darkness. When he came to the opposite bank, Raven asked them to take him across, but they would not. Then he said to them, "If you don't come over I will have daylight break on you." But they answered, "Where are you from? Do you come from far up the Nass where lives the man who has daylight?" At this Raven opened his box just a little and shed so great a light on them that they were nearly thrown down. He shut it quickly, but they quarreled with him so much from across the creek that he became angry and opened the box completely, and the sun flew up into the sky. The people who wore sea-otter or fur-seal skins, or the skins of any other sea animals, went into the ocean, while those with land-otter, bear, or marten skins, or the skins of any other land animals, went into the woods, and became the animals and sea creatures whose skins they wore."

(Adapted from: Tlingit Myths and Texts by John R. Swanton. Bureau of American Ethnology Bulletin 39, Smithsonian Institution, Washington, D.C. 1909. Myth recorded at Sitka, Alaska, 1904)

THE LAND THAT RAVEN MADE

The lands and rivers created by the marvelous Raven are now called the Northwest Coast of North America. Geologists and paleontologists have their stories of creation, but they are not nearly as colorful as the adventures of Raven. Geologists say that the mountains and landforms are terranes--remnant pieces of ancient continents that have pushed to this northern shore. These parcels of land are very old. They are a continuation of the Coast Mountain Range which extends along the western edge of North America. In many places, the mountains rise directly from the sea. Ascending from sea level to 10,000 feet or more, some of the mountains are batholiths which arose in the Mesozoic Age while others are volcanoes, such as Mount Edgecumbe. There have been recent eruptions of other volcanoes. For example, on the night of August 24, 1775, the Spanish explorers rested in Bucareli Bay, just south of the present town of Craig. They reported that there was a volcano erupting four or five times a day and that it lit up the entire night sky. We are not sure where the eruption occurred, but it shows that this is a young and growing land.

Deep fault lines parallel the coast. For instance, Chatham Strait is more than 1500 feet deep in many places. Chatham Strait and Lynn Canal form one of the longest fjords in the world. The Panhandle, as southeastern Alaska is called, is only 250 miles long with a multitude of bays, inlets and channels. It has a shoreline of more than 11,000 miles--as much as the rest of the continental United States!

During the ice ages, rivers of ice cut through the mountain ranges and pushed out to the sea. At the height of the last glaciation, 20,000 years ago, the land upon which Juneau is built was buried under 2,000 feet of ice. Ten thousand years ago, the last major ice age ended. With the weight of ice removed, the land has continued to rise. Juneau has the greatest rate of uplift of any place in the world. Old beaches, with their rocks and sea shells, can now be found more than 400 feet above the present high tide. After a warming trend of a few thousand years, a cooler period known as the "Little Ice Age" set in. This lasted from about 2500 to 200 years ago. When Vancouver's men rowed down Icy Strait in 1794, there was no Glacier Bay. The face of the glaciers were near the edge of Icy Strait. Today, the glaciers have retreated more than fifty miles. Tlingit oral history tells of the days when the face of the Mendenhall Glacier was at the Gastineau Channel, more than two miles from where it is today.

Famous for its incessant rains, Southeastern Alaska is a northern rain forest. A combination of factors creates the rare ecosystem found in this area. The jet stream, passing over the South Pacific, picks up warm, moist air and carries it to the Northwest Coast. The clouds rising over the coastal mountains drop their moisture on the land below, creating the rain forest. The average rainfall for all of Southeastern is 65 inches a year. The minimum precipitation is 11 inches, while some places, such as Little Port Walter, receive 200 inches of rain a year. The weather is generally determined by two semipermanent atmospheric weather systems. During the summer, the North Pacific High, whose center lies off the California coast, widens and carries warm air northward. In the winter, the Aleutian Low expands, bringing colder weather to the coast. In the Pacific Ocean, part of the Subarctic Current also carries warmer water northward along the coast of the Panhandle during the summer months. As a result, the weather in this region is neither as hot nor as cold as it is in the interior regions to the north. The heavy rainfall creates thousands of streams and rivers which are the nurseries for five species of salmon.

This part of the world also has extreme tides. Every six and a half hours, the tides may rise or fall as much as twenty feet, averaging more than three feet an hour. There are strong tidal currents. In narrow openings, the waters occasionally rush through at a speed of eleven miles an hour. Long ago, the Tlingit learned to take advantage of these currents for fishing and travel.

There are annual variations in the weather. If high pressure systems develop over the mainland in Canada, the cool, dry, inland air flows over the mountains to the coast. This flow brings cool, clear days in summer and windy, cold, bright days in winter.

In an exceptionally cold winter, the temperature may drop as low as twenty degrees below zero for several days. The next winter might be so warm that there is no snow, just rain. Summers are generally warm. Normally the daylight temperature will rise to 70° F in July. In a rare, hot summer, the temperature may reach 80° F for several days. For example, in the summer of 1987, it was hot and dry for six weeks; some places had no rain for this entire time. Alaska is sometimes called the "Land of the Midnight Sun." But that is true only for the northern part of the state in the summer time. In Sitka, for example, during June and July the sun rises about 4:00 a.m. and sets about 10:00 p.m. But in the months of December and January, sunrise is about 8:30 a.m. and sets again near 4:00 p.m. These changes in temperature and daylight dictate much of daily life. While summer is the time for fishing and intense activity, winter is the time for social gatherings and celebrations. It was also the time for making clothing, tools, utensils and weapons. It is an age-old cycle.

Daily winds change with the seasons. In the summer, there are a few storms. On a hot summer day, the afternoon pressure system causes strong westerly winds to build, creating waves up to six feet high. In the winter, when a high pressure system builds over Canada and flows into Southeastern, the winds may increase to fifty miles an hour and the waves rise to ten or twelve feet. In the winter, temperatures can range anywhere from twenty degrees above to twenty degrees below zero. In the ancient past, it is said that the Tlingit avoided winter travel. But in the summer, they traveled up and down the "inside waters" from what is now the town of Haines to the Seattle area. The neighboring Haida, called "The Vikings of the Northwest Coast," traveled the open seas winter and summer on their voyages of trade and war.

The Northwest Coast was a bountiful place to live for those who had the skills to survive. Sometimes the weather was good, sometimes dangerous. There were good years and bad years. But through them all, the Tlingit achieved a detailed knowledge of their country in all of its changing moods. It was the knowledge, skills and determination which enabled them to develop one of the great cultures of aboriginal America.

PLANTS AND ANIMALS OF TLINGIT COUNTRY
RAVEN CREATES FISH

One day, Raven called the salmon together to choose their rivers. King Salmon said "I will travel up the long, large rivers to the clear waters, where I will spawn." Dog Salmon was next. "I, too, want the larger rivers," he said, "but if they are filled, I will use the smaller streams." Next came Coho. "I prefer the short, fast, clear waters for my spawning," was his request. Sockeye was quick to step up and said, "I claim the lakes." At the end was poor little Humpback. He looked up and softly said, "I'll take whatever is left." And so it is that even today, each type of salmon can be found in the streams they picked. But you will notice that there are more Humpback salmon than all the others.

(Adapted from a legend told by Walter Williams, Tlingit storyteller.)

The Northwest Coast of North America is rich in natural resources. Before the arrival of the first European explorers, the region supported a large Native population. The abundance of Pacific salmon (Oncorhynchus) allowed the Tlingit to develop a rich, complex society. Chart I shows that each species of salmon has its own life cycle, spawning areas and food value. At the end of each cycle, the salmon come back from the ocean to spawn and it was at this time that the Indians caught them. If one species of salmon had a low return in a particular year, it was quite likely that some other species had a larger run. The Indians who lived near several kinds of salmon streams could expect a good supply of salmon every year. In northern California, there were small runs of salmon for several months each year. To the north, the runs were larger. At Bristol Bay and in the rivers of western Alaska, there were huge returns of salmon, but in the past, the problem was that they all returned at one time and the people were unable to dry enough fish in a short time to feed themselves throughout the winter. From Seattle to Yakutat, however, the salmon runs continued for about three months, from July through September. Here, each family was able to preserve enough salmon to provide for most of the winter. Dried salmon was the mainstay of their diet.

Most salmon were caught by building fences or weirs across the streams and placing a basket trap in an opening in the fence so that the salmon trying to get upstream guided into the trap. At other times, salmon were gaffed or caught in nets as they entered the freshwater streams to spawn.

When the Pacific herring came to the shore to spawn in late winter and early spring, the Indians harvested their eggs, or "roe." Normally, the herring laid their eggs on rocks and seaweeds. The Indians gathered the seaweed with the roe on it. Another way to harvest the eggs was to put hemlock branches in the water, letting the herring lay their eggs on them. Then the Indians pulled the branches out of the water and peeled off the eggs. When people wanted both the herring and the eggs they built a semicircular stone wall along the shore. At high tide the fish were able to swim over the barrier, but as the tide went out, they were trapped behind the wall. The Tlingit scooped up the herring with a large, paddle-like tool which had sharp spines along its edge. Sweeping this rake through the water, they impaled several herring and then shook them off into their canoes. These stone weir traps were also built at the mouths of streams to catch salmon as they milled around in front of their spawning streams.

Another favorite food on the Northwest Coast was the oil from the Eulachon, also called "hooligan" or "candlefish." The term "candlefish" comes from the fact that after they are dried, they can be burned for light like a candle. Eulachon oil was not only used for eating, it was also a precious trade item. Some Natives still call it "liquid gold."

CHART I
Pacific Salmon (Oncorhynchus)

COMMON NAME				
King	Silver	Chum	Sockeye	Pink

SCIENTIFIC NAME				
O.Shawytscha,	O.Kisutch	O.Keta	O.Nerka	O.Gorbuscha

OTHER NAMES				
Chinook, Tyee	Coho	Dog	Red	Humpback

BEGINNING OF UPSTREAM MIGRATION				
May & Aug.	July-Aug.	Aug-Sept.	June-Aug.	July-Sept.

PRINCIPAL SPANWNING MONTHS				
July & Sept.	Sept.-Oct.	Sept.-Oct	June-Sept.	July-Sept.

YOUNG REMAIN IN FRESH WATER				
1-2 years	1-2 years	days-6 months	6 months lake 1-3 yrs.	days- months

LENGTH OF OCEAN LIFE				
1-5 years	1-2 years	1/2 -4 years	1-4 years	1 year

AGE AT MATURITY				
2-8 years	2-4 years	2-5 years	3-7 years	2 years

LENGTH AT MATURITY IN INCHES				
16-60	17-36	17-38	15-33	14-30
Average: 36	24	25	25	20

WEIGHT AT MATURITY IN POUNDS				
3-125	3-30	3-45	3-30	2-9
Average: 22	10	9	6	4

Halibut were also an important part of the Tlingit diet. These fish can reach six feet in length and weigh more than 400 pounds. The Indians of the Northwest Coast made special hooks for the halibut. These hooks looked like a large "V" turned on its side. Other halibut hooks were shaped like an open circle. Today, many commercial fishermen have rediscovered this old design for their fish hooks. The halibut were eaten fresh or dried for winter food. For many modern Tlingit, dried salmon or halibut is still considered "real" food.

In addition to fishing, Tlingit hunted seals and sea lions. The seals provided not only a rich, dark meat, but more importantly, seal oil was also used for cooking and eating in much the same way that Europeans use butter and cooking oils. The people of Yakutat reportedly ate whale meat if a dead whale washed ashore. It is not certain whether or not they actually hunted whales.

The Tlingit ate many shellfish. Several types of clams, mussels, abalone and cockles were harvested. From the abandoned campsites that have been found, it is clear that these shellfish have been an important food source for thousands of years. The people knew about paralytic shellfish poisoning (PSP) and did not eat clams and cockles in the warm months when the poison is most common. The small chitons known locally as "gum boot," were pried from the rocks at low tide. The chiton, unlike clams and mussels, is not affected by the "red tide," and so can be eaten year round.

Another important food source were the various sea vegetables. Large algae or "kelp" were cooked and mixed with other foods. A smaller plant, today called "black seaweed," is still eaten by many Tlingit and is a rich source of vitamins and minerals.

9

The forests provided other foods from the land such as deer, bear, mountain sheep and goats, and a few smaller animals. Coastal people traveling over the mountain trails to the interior traded for moose and caribou hides and antlers to be made into clothing and tools. The women and young girls gathered roots and bark for weaving, and large amounts of strawberries, raspberries and service berries. Many other plants were eaten while some were used for medicine. At a winter feast, the host was expected to set out huge trays of berries for the guests. Soapberries were considered a great delicacy. They were prepared by whipping them to a froth, and the people ate them by sucking them up loudly from a spoon.

The Indians of the Northwest Coast had an abundant, nutritious diet. The protein of the fish and sea mammals was balanced with the plants and other foods. Salmon are especially rich in vitamins A, B and D. Seal oil supplies 3,500 calories per pound. The berries, sea vegetables and fish eggs were also good sources of vitamin C. The Indian diet was one of the healthiest in the world. As a result, the Tlingit were some of the largest of the North American Indians; many explorers said that some men were over six feet tall.

Southeastern Alaska was, and still is, a horn of plenty for those who had the knowledge and skills to use it. The people had a great understanding of their environment. It was this combination of resources and the ability to use them that enabled the Tlingit to be so successful. Much of the information about the use and value of each plant or animal has been lost, but recently some of it has been recorded by the elders.

CHART II

PARTIAL LIST OF TLINGIT RESOURCES

Fish	Shellfish/Seafood	Sea Mammals
Salmon	Clams	Seals
King	Razor	Sea Lions
Silver	Butter	Porpoises
Chum	Steamer	Sea Otters
Humpback	Horse	Whales
Sockeye	Surf	
Trout	Cockles	
Halibut	Abalone	
Cod	Mussels	
Herring	Chiton	
Eulachon	Dungeness Crab	
Sculpin	Squid	
Red Snapper		

Land Animals

		Birds
Deer	Marmot	Ducks
Mountain Goat	Squirrel	Mallard
Mountain Sheep	Wolf	Pin Tail
Moose	Fox	Widgeon
Bear	Wolverine	Geese
Porcupine	Land Otter	Swans
Beaver	Mink	Cranes
Muskrat	Marten	Eagles
Lynx	Weasel	Ptarmigan
Rabbit	Sea Gulls	Grouse

Berries	Small Plants	Trees
Cranberries	Wild Celery	Spruce
High/Low Bush	Wild Rhubarb	Hemlock
Soapberries	Lupine	Alder
Salmonberries	Black Seaweed	Cedar
Huckleberries	Algae Seaweed	Red/ Yellow
Serviceberries	Skunk Cabbage	Willow
Elderberries	Devil's Club	Crab Apple
Blue Currant		Birch
Nagoon (Lagoon Berries)		Fir
Thimbleberries,		Jack Pine
Swamberries,		
Strawberries	Cultivated Tobacco	

Origins

How Raven Made People

One day Raven felt lonely, so he decided to make people. He strutted along the beach looking for a way to make humans. He saw some stones. He piled them up and said, "Now, become human and walk." The stones started to tremble but they quickly tumbled to the ground. "Well, that didn't work," he said to himself. Then he found some interesting looking sticks and tied them together with grass. Again he said, "Become human and walk!" With only a few clumsy steps they came apart and fell down. Finally he noticed the beach grass ("chook") blowing in the wind. It almost looked alive. He grabbed a handful, tied some across to make the arms and legs and shouted "Walk!" Suddenly it came alive and began to move. Sure enough, that was the first person in the world.

You know, that may be one reason why today some so-called leaders lean one way or the other, depending on how the winds blow!

(Abridged version of story told by Walter Williams, Tlingit Storyteller, member of the Chookaneidi clan.)

ARCHAEOLOGICAL INFORMATION

Archaeologists are not certain when the first people migrated into the New World, although some are convinced that the first Americans came across the Bering Land Bridge more than 30,000 years ago. There is no doubt that Alaska was occupied 10,000 years ago since several archaeological sites can be dated to at least that age

Until the 1960s, the only archaeological sites in Southeastern Alaska were those dating back three or four hundred years. Then in 1968, Dr. Robert Ackerman excavated a site just west of Juneau which proved that someone had camped there more than 9,000 years ago. Since the discovery of this campsite, now known as the

Groundhog Bay site, several more ancient sites have been uncovered. The Hidden Falls site on Baranof Island, east of Sitka, was occupied about the same time as Groundhog Bay. Farther south, on Heceta Island, Ackerman excavated an old shell dump, or midden, that has been carbon-dated to be 8,000 years old.

Nearly all remain are broken and discarded tools along with the shells and bones of the animals consumed. However, a few remains of an early ihabitant has been found in a cave and it has been carbon-dated to 9,980 years ago. There is no way to determine what language these first inhabitants spoke, what their beliefs were, or even what type of society they had. However, some inferences can be made on the basis of the finds so far.

The earliest inhabitants were more than likely a maritime people who traveled, hunted and fished off shore using small wood or skin-covered boats or canoes. The people who camped at Warm Chuck Lake on Heceta Island consumed large amounts of clams, cockles and other shellfish. From the fish bones in the site, it seems that they fished offshore for halibut, cod and other bottom fish, but also caught some salmon. There are a few bones from land animals, indicating the people were also using the inland areas. So far, no old campsites have been discovered inland, but if any are found, they may throw new light on the total subsistence pattern and culture of these first inhabitants.

The tools from these sites show that these early inhabitants were highly skilled craftsmen. The stone tools from this early period were made from stones that fractured with sharp cutting edges. While many of these tools are rather large, another common type of tool is the small "microblades," sometimes only a quarter inch wide and an inch long. Since stone tools were made in traditional ways, they can be used to identify cultural ties, and hopefully archaeologists will eventually be able to find cultural connections between Southeastern Alaska and other parts of the world.

1.(Photo courtesy of Alaska State Museum. Items # II-B, 224; 205; 130; 221; 142)   Stone implements made by pecking and grinding.

Some of the obsidian found at these earliest sites in Southeastern Alaska came from Mount Edziza about 150 miles inland in British Columbia, showing that for thousands of years people have traveled or traded over long distances on the Northwest Coast.

About 6,500 to 5,000 years ago, a shift in stone tool technology appears, which may indicate a cultural change as well. Yet from the animals remains, it is clear that the people continued to rely on the sea and shoreline for much of their food. Then, between 5,000 and 3,000 years ago, microblades were generally replaced by new tool styles, and lip plugs or "labrets" appear in the sites. While people continued to use flake tools for work which required a very sharp cutting edge, other implements were made from slate which was cut and polished to provide very sharp points and edges. At the same time, there are signs of a greater use of salmon. Archaeologists have found hundreds of large fish traps and weirs, or pounds, to catch salmon as they milled in front of spawning streams. The presence of harpoons tells us that the people continued to hunt sea mammals, while bones from mountain goat, bear, beaver, marmot and muskrat tell us that inland hunting continued. As these early inhabitants developed more advanced techniques, learning to peck and grind harder types of stone into tools that were especially useful for woodworking. They probably used these new tools to carve dugout canoes, make bentwood boxes and construct large plank clan houses. By the time the first Europeans arrived on the coast, the Tlingit had an elaborate stone tool kit, including adzes, hammer stones, wedges, awls, scrapers, blades, net sinkers and arrow and spear points. Tlingit used copper and iron. The copper appears to have come from the Copper River area, but the source of the iron is still uncertain. In more recent sites, archaeologists find that in addition to stone tools, the hunters and gatherers made many other implements from shell, bone, antler, wood and bark. But in the wet acidic soil, the less durable artifacts such as baskets are seldom preserved. However, in 1994, a well-preserved, 5,000 year-old, spruce root basket was discovered on the banks of the Thorne River.

Archaeological evidence from farther south on the Northwest Coast, in the Seattle-Vancouver area, indicates that what is now known as the Northwest Coast art form had its beginning there nearly 3,000 years ago. The stone tools and other objects from this time period suggest that the Northwest Coast cultural tradition was expanding into Southeastern Alaska. The Indians of the Northwest Coast produced sophisticated and elaborate works of art. For example, many of their pecked-and-ground tools were carved with human faces and crest designs. Skilled craftsmen even produced animal and human figurines from stone. Traditionally, the Tlingit and Haida shared in the Northwest Coast art tradition. A few of the famous stories relating the adventures of Raven describe his earliest activities on the Nass River in what is now British Columbia. These legends may be a clue to the historical migrations of the people. By the time the first Europeans arrived, the Tlingit had apparently been here a very long time, had a highly organized society and shared in the Northwest Coast cultural lifestyle.

The population seems to have increased. In Tebenkof Bay alone, archaeologist Herb Maschner found over 150 campsites. The building of large, permanent winter homes, the use of labrets, the presence of finely made ornaments and ceremonial items, all seem to reflect a change in the social structure with increased concern with rank, prestige and family wealth. By 1,500 years ago, fortified sites or protected sites, called "noo" in Tlingit, were common and their number seems to have increased dramatically between 900 and 1,400 A.D.

Although no one knows what language the people spoke as they used these tools, it is probable that by this time the people of Southeastern were speaking Tlingit.

Many carved rocks, or petroglyphs, are found along the shoreline, but since they cannot be dated by any technique known today, we are unable to determine who made them or when they were carved. However, a few of them depict sailing ships, and so, they must have been carved after the arrival of European traders.

2.(Photo courtesy of the Alaska State Museum. Item #II-B 1194) Carved stone figure of a fish, but if it is turned vertically, it appears as a human face.

Who were these first inhabitants? Were theyTlingit or Haida? Archaeologists cannot answer these questions yet.

One theory is that an early group of immigrants came along the coast leaving behind the 8,000 to 10,000 year-old sites. Later on, the ancestors of the Tlingit arrived. It may be that the first coastal Tlingit met the earlier immigrants and either intermarried or drove them out. Another theory is that these earliest hunters and fishermen were really the ancestors of the Tlingit.

Tlingit oral history contains stories and legends describing how the people came to the coast. Several of these accounts tell how they came down from the interior, passed under a glacier, and then reached tidewater. Eventually, different clans spread out to new locations. Finally, all of Southeastern Alaska became Tlingit territory.

The other inhabitants of Southeastern, the Haida, speak an entirely different language. We know that their homeland was in the Queen Charlotte Islands and that they moved into Alaska within the past two to three hundred years. In the late 1880s, a group of Tsimshian Indians, led by Rev. William Duncan, settled at Metlakatla on Annette Island, near Ketchikan. They were given the island as a reservation, and so today they have the only true Indian reservation in Alaska.

Southeastern Alaskan archaeology is still in its infancy. This is one of the most difficult places in the world to locate and excavate archaeological sites. The alternating cold and warm weather, the heavy rainfall, the acidic soil, and the rapid reforestation all contribute to the disappearance of most remains. In only a few decades, abandoned villages are completely overgrown. After several hundred years, only stone tools and a few bones remain. As a result of Ackerman's studies and the work of Forest Service archaeologists, a number of cultural patterns are beginning to emerge. As more and more sites are discovered, there are as many new questions as there are answers concerning the prehistory of Southeastern Alaska. Linguists are now studying the language to determine its relationship to Athabaskan. Perhaps someday the linguists, archaeologists and Tlingit tradition bearers will be able to put together a more complete picture of the origins of the Tlingit people.

INLAND TLINGIT

Today there are a few Tlingit settlements in northern British Columbia and southern Yukon Territory. In historic times, there was a great deal of trade between the coastal and interior Tlingit and neighboring Athabaskan-speaking peoples. Dr. Catherine McClellan has spent many years researching the culture and history of these people. She feels that these Tlingit-speaking people of the interior may be descendants of Tlingit who ventured up the rivers and through the mountain passes from the coast to obtain furs for trade with the Europeans. Another possibility is that they are descendants of people who originally spoke one of the Athapaskan languages, but then adopted Tlingit both as their trade and everyday language. Some of those living along the Taku River, which flows from British Columbia into Stephens Passage just south of Juneau, moved farther inland when the boundary was drawn between Alaska and Canada.

Living east of the Alaska mountain range in a continental climate, the Inland Tlingit have different resources than their coastal relatives. For instance, although they don't catch sea mammals or fish such as halibut and flounder, they are able to hunt moose, caribou, lynx, rabbits and other food sources that are normally not found on the coast. The winters can be much colder, but the summers are warmer and there is much less precipitation on the eastern side of the mountains. Because of the climate and resources, much of their technology and diet were similar to that of the nearby Athabaskans.

The Inland Tlingit preserved the social system of the coastal Tlingit with its matrilineal moiety system and clans with crests. In addition, the interior people share many of the myths and legends, artistic designs, songs and dances of their coastal cousins. Even today, many of the Native place names for geographic features are derived from the Tlingit language. In fact, since the time that written records have been kept, there has continued to be intermarriage and exchange between coastal and interior Tlingit. But since they are not American citizens, they have not shared in the Alaska Native Land Claims and are just now arriving at their own settlement with the Canadian government.

From here on, the description will focus on Alaska, coastal Tlingit, but the reader should keep in mind that there are differences with the Inland Tlingit.

Language

The Tlingit language, like other languages, has its own sound system, vocabulary and grammar. A speaker of English will discover that Tlingit has many sounds not used in English, and in return lacks some sounds in the English language. In a general way, one can say that Tlingit has many more "back" sounds than English, and there are no frontal sounds such as the ones we usually write with a "b," "p," or "m." Since many of the sounds of Tlingit are unlike any European language, the early recordings of the language vary from writer to writer.

The difference in sound systems accounts for the fact that most non-Tlingit pronounce the opening sounds of the word "Tlingit" with a sound like the English "k." To pronounce the word "Tlingit" properly, one has to place the tongue as if to say the opening sound of "love" or "like." Then, without vibrating the vocal cords, allow the air to flow out either side of the tongue. The result sounds like a lisp in English, but is a distinct unit of the Tlingit language. The term "Tlingit" means either a person or people, so it is both a singular and plural term, and at the same time refers to their language.

Tlingit also has a different way of forming words and sentences than English. For example, English modifiers may come before or after the basic verb. Tlingit usually places all modifiers before the verb stem. These modifiers allow Tlingit to express a wide range of meanings. The language can explain abstract concepts as well as the English language. Analyses of Tlingit oratory at memorials for the dead show that the elderly people are still able to develop extended metaphors in their extemporaneous speeches. It is a highly specialized art form. The first speaker highlights an event from the history of the host clan, using metaphors to illustrate the importance of the event. Following speakers expand on the comparison, using the same style and metaphors.

To a certain extent, people view the world through their language. A single comparison can illustrate the differences. In English, the word for the common weed with the yellow top is dandelion. The term comes from the French "dent de lion," or "teeth of the lion." The Tlingit name for this same plant translates into "Raven's basket." The difference is due to the fact that English-speaking people look at the plant when it is in bloom and the petals of the flower look like lion's teeth. The Tlingit look at the plant as it goes to seed, and the cluster of seeds appear like a basket which Raven left unfinished. Both groups are looking at the same "reality," but from different points of view. This one example shows that to really understand another culture, a person must understand its language and way of seeing the world.

There was no accepted system for writing Tlingit until the 1960's when Constance Naish and Gillian Story published a Tlingit noun dictionary. Since then, there have been some modifications made to their system, and it has now become the accepted way of recording and writing the language. This writing system uses the standard characters found on a regular typewriter. However, the characters don't always have the same pronunciation as they have in English. The underlining and apostrophes all indicate special types of sounds found in Tlingit. Those wishing to learn to speak the language, cannot do so simply by reading about it. They must hear a fluent speaker of the language pronounce it correctly and then try to copy the sounds. The Alaska Native Language Center at the University of Alaska Fairbanks and the Sealaska Heritage Foundation in Juneau have now published several works in Tlingit using the new writing system. Presently, there are efforts being taken to record many old stories and oral narratives before the elderly people die.

Most young Tlingit do not speak their language, but some are learning a few words and phrases in school as part of the Native studies program. It appears that before long only a handful of people will be fluent speakers of the language.

While non-Native generally name places for specific individuals, Tlingit nearly always named places based on their appearance or from historic events. For instance, the Tlingit name for the downtown Juneau area is Dzantik' heeni, means the place where the flounder (who live on sloping sandy beaches) are in fresh water from "Gold Creek." Their name for Glacier Bay describes a place where the glaciers are being replaced by water.

COUNTING IN TLINGIT

tléix' - one

déix - two

nás'k - three

daax'oon - four

tleidooshú - six

daxadooshú - seven

nas'gadooshú - eight

gooshúk - nine

jinkaat (hands of a man) - ten

jinkaat ka tléix' - eleven

tleikáa (one person) - twenty

tleikáa ka tléix' - twenty-one

tléixnax káa - one person

dáxnáx káa - two people

tléix' dahéen (tlédaheen) - once

déix dahéen (daxdahéen) - twice

View of the Warm Chuck area, Heceta Island. Within the area shown, archaeologists have found an 8,000 year old campsite; 5-6,000 year old shell midden; a rock shelter occupied 4,000 years ago; a village site inhabited from about 1400-1900 a.d.; stone fish weir with a complex petroglyph. Roads were cut for clear cut logging in the 1980s. (Photo by Wallace Olson)

Bentwood box. Sides were formed by grooving a board and then steaming and bending it into a rectangle. The sides are painted and opercula shells inserted on the top edges. One corner and the bottom are secured with wooden pegs. (Photo courtesy Alaska State Museum, Item # II-B-1124)

Material Culture

VILLAGES, TOOLS AND TECHNOLOGY

The plentiful resources supported a large Tlingit population. There have been several estimates of the aboriginal population at the time of contact with Europeans. The nineteenth century census reports give the population as 8,000 to 10,000 people. But these reports were made only after many epidemics had swept through the region. Smallpox appears to have been introduced as early as 1774. The great epidemic of 1836 may have killed off half of the people in the villages.

There are some clues as to the prehistoric population. The many large shell middens, the complex social organization, the multitude of settlements in hundreds of small bays and inlets, the abundance of resources, all suggest that there was a large population. Although many scholars give the population at 10,000 to 15,000 at the beginning of historic times, the actual number may have been twice as many.

The Tlingit homeland can be divided into large territories known as "kwáans." The term means "people of that place." For example, if someone living just north of Juneau at Auke Bay were asked where he or she were from, they would reply "Aak'w kwáan." The linguist, Jeff Leer, has identified eighteen former kwáan regions. In more recent times, the small kwáans have been absorbed into the larger ones, or are no longer distinguished as separate groups. Today, most people speak of twelve kwáans. From north to south, they are called Yakutat, Chilkat, Sitka, Hoonah, Auke, Taku, Stikine, Kake, Angoon, Henya, Sanya and Tongass. The map and key in the front of this book (see pages i and ii) shows the current divisions, the proper transcription of the old names, the modern names, the present settlements and the village corporations formed under the Alaska Native Claims Settlement Act of 1971. Within each kwáan district were permanent settlements. Today there is usually one large village in each kwáan. For example, we find the villages of Hoonah, Kake, or Yakutat in their traditional kwáans. A close study of the old patterns suggests that perhaps 200 years ago the people were more dispersed. It may be that in those times, each large family or clan had its own territories. The movement into the large, central villages might be a more recent event. The selection of a village site depended upon several factors. The site had to be protected from storms, have a clear, sloping beach, be near to salmon streams and other resources, and have good visibility in case of approaching attackers.

The traditional historic Tlingit village consisted of several large wooden clan houses with some smaller structures behind the main buildings. The houses were homes to the members of a large, extended family known as a clan segment or lineage. These winter houses could be up to 50 or 60 feet in length and 20 to 40 feet wide. They were constructed with upright supports which supported the roof and upper wall beams. The whole framework was then covered with large planks. There was one smoke hole on the roof. The single door usually faced the shore, while the end opposite the door was reserved as the living space for the spokesman of the house and his family. The other members of the household lived along the sides of the buildings according to their rank within the family. The lowest ranking individuals and slaves had to be satisfied with a little space near the door. There was one large fireplace for the entire household directly below the smoke hole in the roof.

The upright posts and the wooden screen in front of the spokesman's quarters were decorated with clan crest designs. The upright posts were usually carved or had carved panels put over them. The earliest explorers do not mention seeing many totem poles. They do report that the interior posts were decorated. It may be that it was only after the Indians had metal woodworking tools that totem poles became a popular form of expression.

The houses were so important in Tlingit thought that each was given a special name. The Tlingit word for the building itself is " hit." The spokesman of the house was the "hit saati." Another word that is translated into English as "house" is the Tlingit word "taan." In fact, the word "taan" at the end of a clan name really means "people of the house of...." For example, the name Kaagwaantaan literally means "people of the burned-down house." Deisheetaan are people of the "far out" house. People and even clans were identified by the names of their winter houses.

The summer dwellings were much more simple. These shelters oftentimes consisted of a simple lean-to of planks or barks; they were used by the family at their salmon streams as a temporary residence. At the summer camp, they fished for salmon, picked berries and carried on other gathering activities involved in putting up food for the winter. When they traveled for hunting, trading, or warfare, the people used very crude shelters or simply slept in their canoes.

Although a typical Tlingit winter house could be used as a fortress in case of attack, there were actual fortified settlements and buildings known by the term "noo." Both the Spaniards and Russians described some of these specialized fortresses. The term shows up in some Tlingit names. For instance, Xutsnoowú is literally translated as "fortress of the grizzly bear."

The people were excellent craftsmen. They were particularly good at woodworking. In addition to the houses, their canoes were really great works of applied art and technology. They had a variety of canoes ranging in size from the small, one-man types to the large war canoes which could carry up to thirty or more warriors. Hewn from a single log such as a large red cedar, these large, ocean going canoes were truly impressive. The external shape had to cut the water smoothly and safely while at the same time, the sides had to be thin enough to be pliable and thick enough to provide strength and support. Only a highly skilled carver was able to make a large canoe. Their southern neighbors, the Haida, were blessed with stands of huge red cedar and were master woodworkers. The Tlingit often obtained large Haida canoes in trade and warfare.

The Tlingit had a remarkable collection of tools. Some were used for hunting and fishing, others for construction and warfare, many for food preparation, and others for weaving and works of art.

For inland hunting, the men used a variety of snares, traps and deadfalls. Since travel through the heavy forest was so difficult, they had trained hunting dogs to drive deer down to the beach where the hunters could kill them with spears or bows and arrows. In a few places, the men went high up in the mountains to hunt the wild sheep and goats found there. These animals were hunted not only for their delicious meat, but also for their pelts which were used to make the famous Raven's Tail and Chilkat blankets. As mentioned earlier, the Tlingit had special equipment for catching halibut and herring. But in fishing for salmon, they used fish weirs, dams, traps, nets and gaffs. The most efficient means of fishing the spawning streams was to drive posts into the stream bed and then construct a fence to intercept the migrating salmon. The people used a number of different types of fences and traps. If there were a natural depression at the mouth of a stream, this too could be used as a trap by erecting a stone wall. The fish passed over the wall at high tide and were trapped in the shallow water when the tide went out. Once the fish were entrapped, they were then easily gaffed or speared.

Offshore fishing required hooks and lines. A natural fish line was the stem or stipe of the bull kelp. Several stems could be twisted together for extra strength, and added length could be obtained by joining them with a fisherman's knot. In a few places, strips of whale or sea mammal hides were used for lines. Another common type of line on the Northwest Coast was made from the inner bark of the cedar tree. The same material was used to weave fish nets. Stones, sometimes elaborately decorated, were used as net and hook sinkers. Clubs were important when fishing for halibut. As a large halibut came to the surface--sometimes weighing hundreds of pounds--they had to be clubbed to be subdued. Among the Tlingit and Haida, these halibut clubs were often beautifully carved works of art. One of the most impressive features of the old Tlingit culture was the fact that so many utilitarian tools were decorated. Stones for driving pilings into the stream bed, clubs, hooks, canoes, storage boxes--all were given added beauty by painting or carving.

Fish or other foods were usually eaten when fresh. The most common way of cooking was to make a soup or stew by boiling. The ingredients were cut into pieces and put into water. Hot stones were taken from around the fire and dropped into the water to bring it to a boil and as the rocks cooled, new hot rocks were added. Fish and meat were also cooked or roasted over an open fire. Many things were dried, or smoked and dried, for winter use. The smoking was done not so much for flavor, but mainly as a way of keeping insects away during the drying. Occasionally, some foods, such as salmon eggs, were preserved in oil. In the fall, fish eggs and berries were air dried to preserve them.

The summer fish camp was a place of intense activity. The traps had to be built, the fish caught and dried and packed away for the winter. It was also a time for collecting and preserving berries and other plants. This period of hard work was later balanced by the winter leisure time when the people gathered for feasts and ceremonies. If the summer had been productive, in just a few months they were able to set aside their basic food supply for the rest of the year. There were also special seasons of the year for hunting and gathering certain resources. For instance, spring was the time to gather black seaweed and herring eggs, in winter they harvested shellfish and hunted ducks and geese in the summer, when the birds were molting and unable to fly. In May, the women gathered spruce roots and cedar bark for weaving baskets and other household items. Special tools required to shred and prepare the bark and roots. Normally, the tools were made by the men for the women of their family. The women were master weavers of several kinds of material. Some spruce root baskets were so tightly woven that they were used for carrying water and cooking. Even large hats were made from roots or cedar bark. In addition to the mats and other items made from these materials, the Tlingit were famous for their colorful "Chilkat blankets" or ceremonial robes. The warp for these blankets consisted of cedar bark wrapped in wool, while the woof was pure wool. The same technique used in basket weaving was used to weave the large robes which were worn over the shoulders as well as the men's slipover tunic. In the weaving of the Chilkat blanket, each stitch or weave had to be done individually. It is said that it took a woman about a full year of constant work to produce one of these beautiful robes. Interestingly enough, the basic design was painted on a board by a man, and the woman used it as a pattern for the actual weaving. Today there are only a few women who know how to do this type of weaving. The blankets are so rare and expensive that usually they are made on contract and only go to museums, elderly Tlingit or wealthy collectors. Quite a few women, including non-Natives, have learned how to weave the traditional baskets and hats but like the Chilkat blanket, the time it takes to gather the roots and prepare them in addition to the actual weaving makes them very expensive.

3. (Photo courtesy of Alaska State Museum. Item # II-B-1355) Pattern board for a Chilkat blanket.

The daily clothing of the Tlingit was relatively simple considering the climate. Some of the earliest European sketches of the Tlingit show men wearing only an animal skin over one shoulder. Women wore a tunic of tanned hides reaching to the knees, while men wore a skin robe or tunic. In the winter cold, additional robes or coverings were worn for protection. It is said that some women made rain capes and skirts from cedar bark. From the earliest descriptions, the people seem to have gone barefoot most of the time. They had leather boots or moccasins, but because the ground was usually wet, leather boots would not last very long. For the winter months, and for travel to the interior regions where it was colder, the men wore leather boots. They also used leggings to protect the lower part of the legs. Some museums have snowshoes that are said to be Tlingit, but most of them appear to be identical to those of the interior Athabascans and were probably obtained in trade.

The most impressive form of Tlingit dress was the warrior's armor. A complete outfit consisted of a wooden helmet, oftentimes made into an animal or crest design. Below the helmet was a neck piece or visor to protect the man's face. His chest and waist were covered with a leather jacket or tunic over which he wore worn wooden slat armor. The warrior carried a spear or bow and arrow, and in historic times a knife was worn in a sheath and carried over the shoulder. Ready for battle, a Tlingit warrior must have been an impressive sight! The armor was so effective that after the introduction of firearms, they simply added another layer of leather over the armor so the musket balls would not penetrate. The same hunting spears, bows, arrows and knives were also used for warfare. Another weapon in their arsenal was the canoe paddle. These were sharply pointed and were used as spears in hand-to-hand combat in canoes.

All of the early explorers mention that the Tlingit seemed warlike and always ready for combat. At the least provocation, they grabbed their weapons and were on the alert. One has to realize that there were no police, no court systems, no form of government such as we have today. In the olden times, the family was the only protection an individual had. There was continual raiding and warfare along the Northwest Coast and if the Tlingit had not been warlike, they would have been overrun by their neighbors. Of course, they shared the general Northwest Coast cultural pattern and raided far to the north and south in search of revenge, slaves, and booty. According to Tlingit oral history, some war parties went as far south as present day Seattle. As late as the 1790's, the manager of the Shelikov Company, Alexander Baranov, and his men were surprised by a raiding party of Tlingit in the Prince William Sound area. On the other hand, Indians from farther south raided the Tlingit, and so the old stories are filled with tales of battles and heroism.

Like other Indians in this region, the Tlingit were expert woodworkers. Their most valuable source of wood was the red cedar. Cedar is not only strong and durable, it also has a straight grain and can be split lengthwise with wedges. Whole canoes were carved from a single tree. The timbers were used for house construction. By starting a split and then working in wedges, huge planks and timbers were pried out of each log. These were then used for sides and roofing on the houses. Totem poles were carved from cedar. Perhaps the most interesting technique was used in the making of bentwood boxes. To make such a box, a plank was carefully grooved in three places at right angles to the length of the board. The board was then steamed or softened with boiling water and bent on the grooves to make the four sides of a box. The final joining of the two ends at one corner was done with pegs or with a lacing of spruce roots. A separate top and bottom were cut and fitted into place. A well-made box was water-tight and used for the storage of foods, ceremonial goods, and other items. Carvers made many three- dimensional wooden objects. There were bowls, spoons, figurines, rattles, clubs, and dance batons in every Tlingit house. Nearly all of these items were decorated with animal and crest designs. Some of the designs were carved into the wood, and in others the objects were simply painted with a design. Two-dimensional art was done by painting or carving. The wall or screen at the back of the house, separating the spokesman's area from the others, was usually painted.

Another favorite material for art was the horn of the mountain goat or sheep. After the horn was softened by heating in water and shaped into a spoon, the handle was usually decorated with carvings. Besides the wood and antler, the Tlingit used shells such as abalone, teeth and other materials in their art. A long, tubular shell known as <u>dentalia</u> was obtained in trade from Vancouver Island and was a valuable trade item.

The average Tlingit was surrounded by art in his or her everyday life. Works of art were cherished as ceremonial items, and rare objects were acquired in trade and war. Art was so common that today a large portion of the museum collections of Northwest Coast art came from the Tlingit.

From the arrival of the first European traders on the coast, the Tlingit material culture began to change. They were anxious to get firearms, metal tools, and utensils--almost anything that was new and unusual. Most of the early traders describe them as shrewd, hard bargainers. Iron was one of the most popular trade items. The Indians of the Northwest Coast had iron prior to contact with the traders; many experts believe that it must have come from Chinese and Japanese shipwrecks along the coast. In any case, when the early explorers arrived, for example the Spaniards at Bucareli Bay in 1775, the Indians knew exactly what iron was and were willing to trade furs for metal. Many times the traders complained that when they were not watching, the Indians would steal any metal object left unguarded. By 1792, the Tlingit knew how to work and shape iron or steel and copper. The Spaniards at first thought that the Tlingit had obtained their knives in trade, but the Indians explained that they knew how to make their own. The advent of more iron may have touched off a flourish of carving, especially of totem poles. The first explorers seldom mention totem poles, but by the early 1800's they were reportedly seen in every village.

4.(Photo courtesy of Alaska State Museum. Item # II-B-1746) 19th Century Tlingit carved bowl.

One of the most valuable items on the Northwest Coast was the "copper." Sheets of copper were made into a rectangular form, somewhat like a shield and were displayed on important occasions. It is possible that some of these coppers were made prior to contact. Copper nuggets from the Copper River area of Alaska and interior Canada were traded to the coastal people and it was from these that the early coppers were made. But it appears that all of the coppers currently in existence were made from sheets of metal obtained from trade with the Europeans. Early ships had their hulls sheathed in copper to protect them from salt water wood borers. Ships also

33

carried extra sheets of copper for repairs, and this may have been the historic source of the metal.

An interesting example of cultural creativity occurred when the sailors and traders gave the Native people clothing and blankets. Along with large pieces of cloth the Europeans traded buttons. The Indians took the buttons and attached them to their blankets in traditional totemic crest designs. Today these "button blankets" are still being made, but some are more than a hundred years old. A more recent change has been that instead of buttons, beads are used to trim cloth jackets, blankets, and vests. The Russians brought many trade beads during the 19th century, and these old beads are now very valuable.

In the past 200 hundred years, many of the old art forms have changed, and several have disappeared altogether. Today, no one makes stone tools, and only a few people continue to weave, but carving and painting are still popular with many artists. Artists now experiment with new colors and forms while retaining the basic traditions of the past.Many art collectors still seek out Tlingit and other Northwest Coast Indian art.

Social Culture

Every society is organized, but the way people organize themselves differs from culture to culture. In order to understand daily life and culture among the Tlingit, one has to understand the social structure In which it operated. Tlingit society was built upon a few basic principles (Chart III).

First, a person traced his or her relationships through the mother's side of the family. Anthropologists refer to it as a matrilineal system. Such a system is sometimes mistakenly called a "matriarchal" system. The term "matriarchy" means that women control the society or that they are the political leaders. Amongst the Tlingit, women had a great deal of power and influence, but the official spokesman of each house was always a male.

Secondly, Tlingit were divided into two sides, which social scientists refer to as a moiety system, meaning divided in half. Each side was identified by its "crest" or emblem. One side was always known as the Raven side, its opposite was called either the Eagle or the Wolf side. One southern group claimed to be on both sides, but this is really an anomaly because each side had to interact with its opposite in nearly all aspects of social life.

Thirdly, a person was always identified by the family to which he or she belonged. The broadest family groups are technically known as "clans." Clans consider themselves related through a legendary ancestor. Under each side, the Raven and the Eagle, there were at least thirty different clans. Each clan had its own legend of how it originated and why it had a right to use a certain design or crest. For instance, one clan owns the story of the creation of the killerwhale, and through it, has a right to use the killerwhale as its crest. According to Tlingit oral history, clans often divided into new groups, while other clans merged. Each clan had a name and, as mentioned earlier, many of these names were taken from the houses where they originated. Another ending to clan names is the term "-eidee" or "-yadee," which means "people" or "child of.... " For example, there are the Shangukeidee, the L'eeneidee, L'uknax.adee, and the Chookaneidee. Since these names are sometimes difficult for non-speakers of Tlingit to pronounce, many people find it easier to refer to them by the crest or design which a clan uses as its insignia. These crests are sometimes referred to as "totems," but they are not the same as the totems of the Australian aborigines and others who consider themselves as actual children of certain animals or creatures.

There is a problem in using the crest to identify each clan because sometimes a clan has more than one crest, or one crest may be used by more than one clan. For example, one clan in Sitka and another clan in Yakutat both claim the frog as a crest, but each clan's crest has its own separate story or legend to support the family's right to use the design. On the other hand, it appears that at one time several of the clans on the Eagle side were one clan that divided. As a result, the Kaagwaantaan usually use the bear as a clan crest, but some other Eagle groups say that they also have a right to use it. Over the years there have been disputes among clans concerning who has the right to use certain crests. The only accurate way to understand the relationship of the clans and their crests is to learn their clan history from members of that particular clan.

Members of one side oftentimes considered themselves as brothers or sisters to other members of the same side. For example, a person on the Eagle side may refer to others on the Eagle side as a brother or sister. They don't mean that they are biological brothers or sisters, but that socially they see themselves as one side in contrast to those of the opposite side. Anthropologists often use the term "phratry," meaning brotherhood, to describe this feeling of clan relationship.

Clan members often lived in different kwáans, as described earlier. One particular clan might have subdivisions in three or four kwáans. The local subdivision or segment of a clan is usually known as a lineage. While clan members considered themselves related through a legendary ancestor, local lineage members usually knew exactly how they were related to other members of that lineage. They were able to trace their ancestry back through their mother's side to identify precise ties to others. Sometimes, even local lineages became so large that they further divided into separate buildings or houses.

Each winter house had a name which was well known not only by other village members, but also by distant relatives in other kwáans. In a large settlement a person was known by the house in which he or she lived. The members of each large house were all related either through their mothers or by marriage. Slaves were owned by the head of the house and the family, and lived in the family house. The ultimate unit in Tlingit society was the individual. Each person was given a traditional name. The name was extremely important because it reflected one's standing in the family and in the community. Each name belonged to a particular lineage, and others knew who had a right to use certain names. A name was like a cultural passport. If a person were given a prestigious name, he or she was expected to live up to the examples and ideals of previous holders of the name.

THE TLINGIT CALENDAR

The Tlingit calendar was based on the lunar cycle, and so it does not match our modern system of twelve months. There were many local variations. In Tlingit, "dísi" means lunar month. The following is a sample of what a typical calendar was like:

Sha̲xeyí (August) "new snow on mountains" When things get fat.
(meaning unclear) Start of New Year.

Dís yádi (September) Small Moon month End of fish and berries

Dís tléin (October) Big Moon month First snow, bears are fat.

K̲ukahaa dísi (November) (Bear) Dig den month Snow shoveling.

X̲aana̲x dísi (December) Hair develops Animals in the womb begin to have hair.

T'aawá̲k dísi (January) Canadian goose month When sun and geese return.

S'eek dísi (February) Black bear month Young are born.

X'éigaa kayaaní dísi (March) Real flower month Land flowers grow.

Héen táaná̲x kayaaní dísi (April) Blossoms under water month Water plants grow, collect herring eggs.

Jinkaat aa dísi (May) 10th month People know everything will grow.

X̲áat dísi (June) Salmon month Salmon arrive.

Atgada̲xeet dísi (July) Breeding month (animals) Everything is born.

CHART III
SOCIAL STRUCTURE

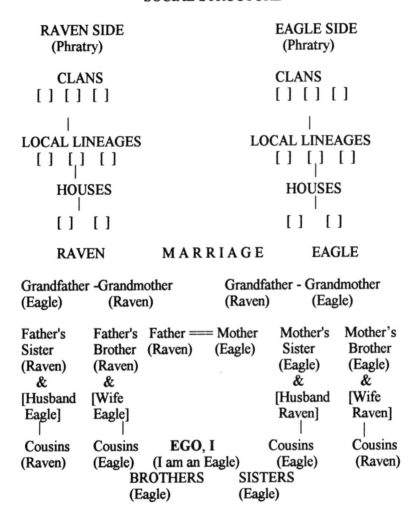

RAVEN SIDE   EAGLE SIDE
(Phratry)   (Phratry)

CLANS   CLANS
[ ] [ ] [ ]   [ ] [ ] [ ]

LOCAL LINEAGES   LOCAL LINEAGES
[ ] [ ] [ ]   [ ] [ ] [ ]

HOUSES   HOUSES

[ ]   [ ]   [ ]   [ ]

RAVEN   M A R R I A G E   EAGLE

Grandfather -Grandmother   Grandfather - Grandmother
(Eagle)   (Raven)   (Raven)   (Eagle)

Father's	Father's	Father === Mother	Mother's	Mother's
Sister	Brother	(Raven) (Eagle)	Sister	Brother
(Raven)	(Raven)		(Eagle)	(Eagle)
&	&		&	&
[Husband	[Wife		[Husband	[Wife
Eagle]	Eagle]		Raven]	Raven]
Cousins	Cousins	EGO, I	Cousins	Cousins
(Raven)	(Eagle)	(I am an Eagle)	(Eagle)	(Raven)

BROTHERS   SISTERS
(Eagle)   (Eagle)

Notice that in this system, if you were the Eagle person (EGO), some of your cousins would be on the same side, others opposite. Your Eagle cousins would be like brothers and sisters. Your Raven cousins would be opposite to you. Your father, as a Raven, would be on the opposite side. You would inherit from your Mother's Brothers and Sisters, not from your Father's side of the family.

Personal identity was traced through one's mother, to house membership, to local lineage, to clan and then to which side one was on, Raven or Eagle/Wolf. Ultimately a person considered himself or herself to be a Tlingit, a real person, as opposed to all outsiders who were not Tlingit.

This entire structure was so well known by traditional Tlingit that by knowing a person's name one automatically knew that he or she belonged to a specific house, lineage and clan.

When the Europeans began to trade on the Northwest Coast, they used terms such as "chief," "tribe," and "nation" to describe the social structure. In fact, there never were any of these concepts present in the old Tlingit culture. There was no "chief" or head man of one side, one clan or even of a whole lineage. The highest ranking person was the spokesman of the house or "hitsaati." In some places, the spokesman of the oldest house of a particular lineage was more influential than others, but he could only speak directly for his house. To become a spokesman, one had to be born into the proper family and then be selected or approved as a spokesman. Usually, the spokesman position was passed along by seniority in a matrilineal fashion. The oldest son of the oldest sister of the spokesman generally took over if he were ambitious, respected and accepted by the members of the household. There was no formal council or vote to direct the spokesman's decision. He knew, of course, how much support or opposition he had, and so he needed to be careful. As the head of the house, the spokesman was also responsible for all of its members. If an outsider attacked or challenged a member of the house, the spokesman was expected to defend his house member. The household and local lineage were the individual's source of security and prestige. A Tlingit was born, raised, lived, and died as the member of a lineage. Without that support the person was an outcast. The strongest insult in Tlingit is to describe someone as a "child of the beach" meaning that he or she has no family, no support, no pride and is unworthy of any respect.

The lineage or house owned or controlled many things including land, songs, stories and works of art. If people wished to fish in a certain stream or pick berries in a specific place, they had to get the permission of the local lineage or house spokesman to do so. Any attempt to steal a lineage or clan's stories or crests was cause for war. As the basic economic unit, the lineage owned everything; the individual owned almost nothing. There was no concept of stealing from within the lineage itself because the canoes, food and equipment were not personal possessions. The spokesman was not the sole owner of the house, the land or the ceremonial items. He was only the caretaker and could only give them away with the approval of his family members. The clan, on the other hand, owned very little. Mainly it had the right to stories, songs, ceremonies and other immaterial things. There was no chief or spokesman for the entire clan. Some individuals were more respected than others, but the highest and ultimate authority was the house spokesman.

The basic principle of Tlingit social organization was that of reciprocity. Whatever one clan or lineage did to another would be repaid. On the positive side, if a house or lineage helped another house or an individual, those helping were eventually repaid. On the negative side, revenge was quickly taken for any insult or injury to even just one member of a house. For example, if a person were killed, their relatives would immediately retaliate by killing someone from the perpetrator's family. Less serious offenses were sometimes settled by payment of goods or works of art.

Marriage was to a member of the opposite side or phratry. That is, a Raven had to marry an Eagle or Wolf, and vice versa. In the past, the attempted marriage of two Ravens or two Eagles was considered incest. Marriage linked the society into a cohesive unit, but the practice may have been stressful for a family since a man was always of the opposite side from his wife and children. They

41

were considered brothers and sisters to each other. Today, these restrictions have been relaxed so that some people marry others from the same side. However, in the past, to do so would have torn the fabric of their society because it would disrupt the practice of reciprocity. Sometimes marriages were used to form an alliance between different kwáans. People were expected to marry individuals of the same social standing.

Within Tlingit society there were three general levels of rank or prestige. On the top were the "children of the land," the "aan yadee." These were the most highly respected people from the most powerful families. The term "aan yadee" has been mistakenly translated as "princess" or "royalty." Perhaps the closest English translation would be, "highly respected people." There was no sharp division within the society; there were many gradations of rank. Below the upper class, or respected ones, were commoners of various levels based upon their position in the family and their accomplishments. The anthropologist, Philip Drucker, liked to refer to the Tlingit as a "calibrated" society in which everyone knew where they stood in relationship to everyone else. No two people were exactly equal.

Slaves purchased in trade or captured in wars and raids were considered outside of the Tlingit social class. Some writers maintain that 10 -20% people were slaves with no rights or privileges and were forced to do the hard, dirty work such as clearing large boulders from the beach and bringing in firewood. If they had a special talent, such as carving, they might be given special consideration. Although slaves were not normally accepted as Tlingit, there were cases in which they could be set free or made an accepted member of the society. For instance, an "aan yadee" girl usually had a slave girl as a companion. When the Tlingit reached maturity, the slave companion could be set free and her children considered as Tlingit. For a Tlingit to be taken as a slave was considered a great insult or disgrace for the family which would do whatever it could to get the person back.

CHART IV
SOME TLINGIT TERMS FOR RELATIVES

du - his, hers, its (possessive)

du shagóon - his ancestor

du léelk'w - his grandparent

du éesh - his father

du aat - his father's sister, female on father's side

du sáni - his father's brother, male on father's side

du tláa - his mother

du tláak'w - his mother's sister

du káak - his mother's brother

du húnxw - his older brother

du kéek' - his younger brother

du dlaak' - his sister

du shátx - her older sister

du kéek'- her younger sister

du éek'- her brother

du yádi - his child

du yátx'i - his children

du dachxán - his grandchild

du káani - his brother-in-law, her sister-in-law

du sháawu - his tribal sister

du xooni - his tribal brother, relative

du xwáayi - her tribal brother

du naa - his or her clan, family

káa, káax'w - man, men

shaawát, sháa - woman, women

lingít, leengít - person

aanyádi, aanyátx'i - high class person, persons

goox - slave

aankáawu - chief, rich person

kwáan - people, a people of...

In the Tlingit language, the terms for relatives are very clear and fit in exactly with the social structure (Chart IV). As a comparison, in English, the term uncle can mean either my father's or mother's brother, or the husband of my father or mother's sister. In Tlingit, there are different terms for a mother's brother ("du kaak") and a father's brother ("du sani"). The mother's younger sister was usually called by a term ("du tlaak'w") which means "little mother." A father's sister was called by a special term ("du aat") and had different responsibilities than one's mother's sister. Since a man had to marry a woman of the opposite side, the father's sister was the ideal person to arrange a marriage for her niece or nephew who had to marry a member of their father's side. The father's sister was of the opposite side and knew who was of equal status. All of these kinship terms give us an indication of the role of relatives in Tlingit life. The extended family provided food, education, protection, support in troubled times, prestige, and position in society. Ownership, disputes, revenge, wealth, the legal system and even religion, were all interwoven into the social system.

The Tlingit had strict laws of ownership. Each lineage or house owned physical things such as buildings and equipment. In addition, they owned non-physical things such as stories, legends, ceremonies, exclusive rights to fish at certain streams, the right to berry patches or other resources, and even the right to certain trails for trading with the interior Indians.

Their legal system was based on the principle of reciprocity and their great concern for rank or prestige. Whatever was done to or for a member of a family had to be repaid. But the repayment had to be matched to the social standing of that individual. For example, if a low-ranking person killed a higher ranking person of the opposite side, the victim's clan or lineage took revenge on the murderer's family. Since the victim's side had lost a high-ranking person, a person of equal rank on the opposite side had to be killed. If there were a killing and the clans wished to avoid a long feud, it was expected that a man of equal rank would volunteer to be killed to settle the debt. He would put on his family's ceremonial clothes, step out of the door of the house and give a long speech recalling how his family had always maintained its honor. He then walked out among the warriors of the opposite side, who killed him with spears. Such a death was considered very honorable. If a killing had been accidental, or if a high-ranking person killed a low-ranking one, the death could be repaid with goods or the rights to certain lands or streams. An unrepaid killing or an unresolved dispute could lead to a feud. Long term feuds could go on for years between members of different kwáans.

There were killings and counter-killings. If they reached the point where both sides wanted peace, they could organize a "deer ceremony." Deer were considered the most peaceful of all animals. A few men on each side were selected as "deer." In a mock battle, the "deer" were captured by their opposites and held prisoner. After four days, the "deer" were set free, and there was a feast to celebrate the peace treaty. By holding the men as hostages and not killing them, both sides indicated that they really wanted a truce.

Other crimes such as rape, adultery, stealing, and even insults could be punished by killing the criminal. Because their legal system was so strict, people were trained to be careful in their speech. Women were warned not to gossip because an insult could lead to war. Many of the early explorers described the Tlingit as being very sensitive or "touchy" about their appearance, the way they were treated, and the respect given them. To act disrespectfully towards a Tlingit was to treat him or her like a slave. Any insult or embarrassment brought dishonor to a house and had to be revenged. The early European explorers report that even a slight insult might lead to serious consequences.

In historic times, many of the fights between Tlingit and Whitemen came about because the newcomers did not understand Tlingit law. For example, any time a Tlingit died, members of the opposite side of the deceased gave presents or gifts to the members

45

of the family to compensate them for the loss of a loved one. In one case, in the 1880's, a Tlingit was killed while working for an American company and so his family demanded blankets in payment for his death. When the company refused to pay, the Indians seized the company boats. The Americans called in the military who bombarded the village.

The real problem was that the Americans could not afford to recognize Tlingit law. If they admitted that the Tlingit had a legal claim to the land, it would be illegal to simply take it away from these original owners. By calling them savages and barbarians, the newcomers rationalized their exploitation. The Euroamericans had superior firepower and could force their ways upon the Indians. It was not until 1924, when Indians were made citizens, that they could take legal action, but by then it was too late--all of their lands and property had been taken away.

Another aspect of Tlingit culture that has caused legal difficulties is the traditional pattern of inheritance. Everything had to remain within the lineage or clan. A man could not pass things on to his children because a man and wife were of opposite clans, and the children belonged to their mother's side. As mentioned earlier, the spokesman was really the custodian of the family's possessions and rights; he was not a sole owner. When a spokesman died, one of his brothers' or sisters' sons had to replace him. In recent times there have been court cases where people claimed personal ownership of artifacts and wanted to sell them. To do so is in conflict with traditional concepts of ownership. Today, legal experts are trying to reconcile the two systems.

Although spokesmen were always male, the earliest explorers all commented on the fact that many times women seemed to be in charge. For example, as the canoes came out to trade, there was usually an old woman sitting in the stern. She made the final decision whether or not to trade. Women arranged marriages and allocated family names to young people. When a spokesman died, the man replacing him was expected to take the widow as a wife.

The idea was that once a woman was married, her husband's family was to support her for the rest of her life. When her husband died, someone else needed to take on those obligations.

This structure and system functioned from generation to generation for at least hundreds of years, and it was within this framework that every individual lived and died.

CHART V
SOME TLINGIT CRESTS

RAVEN CRESTS	EAGLE/ WOLF CRESTS
King Salmon	Killerwhale
Dog Salmon	Shark
Coho Salmon	Porpoise
Humpback Salmon	Hair Seal
Sockeye Salmon	Puffin
Frog	Flicker
Seagull	Brown Bear
Whale	Black Bear
Swan	Hawk
Snail	Thunderbird
Beaver	Iceberg
Woodworm	Mount Edgecumbe
Mount Fairweather	Mountain Goat
Big Dipper	Thunder
Blackskinned Heron	
Mouse	
Mount Saint Elias	
Octopus	
Sculpin	
Petrel	Petrel

THE TLINGIT INDIVIDUAL

The Tlingit had a strong belief in reincarnation. In many cases, they considered an infant to be a deceased family member reborn. Although all children were expected to live up to the cultural ideals of their ancestors, there were different strategies for training boys and girls. The boys were disciplined for strength. In the olden days, a man took his nephews--his sister's sons--to the beach or icy stream to sit in the cold water, and when they came out, they whipped themselves with branches to restore circulation. According to Walter Williams, this practice was intended to toughen them for adult life. The mental discipline was more important than the physical. Tlingit men needed to have strength and determination, along with a disciplined mind to survive the hardships of daily life and warfare. The icy baths were meant to teach them to ignore pain and discomfort and to keep their thoughts fixed on their goals. Besides the physical training, the young boys learned the skills and techniques needed to be a successful hunter, fisherman and warrior. They were taught how to carve and make tools, how to set fish traps and dead falls, how to locate good hunting and fishing sites, how to take care of their canoes and a host of other practical skills. Much of the training consisted of hands-on experience as an apprentice.

Another important form of training was to listen to and remember carefully all of the oral history, legends, and myths. By the time he was a young adult, a man was expected to know his family history, all the ceremonial privileges of his clan, and all of the important rights claimed by his lineage. If he had been chosen as a successor to the spokesman, he was trained to recite the oral history of his family and was expected to live an exemplary life. A young boy was raised by his mother and father until he was about ten or twelve years old. But since all of the men in the house in which the child was born were of the opposite side, it was time for him to be trained by the men of his own clan. He was sent to live with an

Jan Criswell, well known weaver and instructor at the University of Alaska Southeast, is shown weaving the bottom of a new spruce root basket. (Photo by Steve Henrickson)

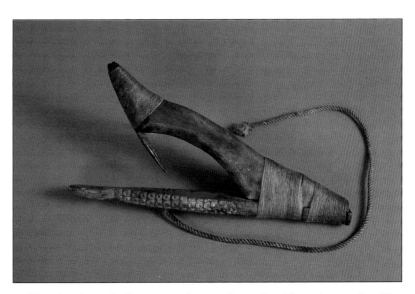

Halibut hook made from two pieces of wood, with an iron point. The pieces are fastened with cord. The lower arm is carved with an octopus design. (Photo courtesy Alaska State Museum. Item # II-B-1524)

uncle, preferably his mother's brother. This is the man who trained and disciplined him as a member of the local lineage. Ideally, he would continue to live in that same house until his death.

Young girls were taught household skills by their mothers and their mothers' sisters. Unlike their brothers, they did not need to move out of their house at puberty because all of the women of the house in which they were born were of the same side. Mothers and aunts both accepted responsibility for the young girls. An upper class girls, an "aan yadee," was always carefully trained and supervised. Chastity was highly prized, and so the old women made sure that these young ladies were virtuous. While out berry picking, for instance, an old woman always acted as chaperon. At puberty, a girl went into isolation in a small building apart from the main house. Ideally, she was isolated for several months, and during that time only small children and older women were allowed to visit her. Her mother and aunts impressed on her the fact that she was no longer a little girl and was soon to be married. Her puberty isolation was publicly known, and so it was also a time for arranging her marriage. Similar forms of puberty isolation are found among many northern peoples.

Most of the marriages for the upper class were arranged from childhood, but some individuals were allowed to choose their marriage partner. If a young man found a girl particularly attractive, he could ask his sisters or mother to arrange the marriage. They then talked with the girl's family to see if the marriage was acceptable to both sides. Generally speaking, clans traditionally intermarried with specific clans of the opposite side. These inter-clan alliances continued over several generations and were often used to form political alliances between clans. When a marriage was agreed upon, the young couple was brought out before the assembled family members of both sides. The two were seated together while a feast was held in their honor. From that point on, they were considered married.

Divorce or separation was very rare, but if a separation did occur, the young children always stayed with the mother. A separation was considered very embarrassing for both families. If a person took his or her own life because of mistreatment by a husband or wife, the offending spouse might be put to death.

As a person grew older, he or she normally rose in prestige and power. The principle of seniority can be traced through the kinship terms and behavior. Elderly people were important treasures of family history and wisdom. They had weathered many of life's storms and that experience was handed on to their descendants through storytelling and teaching.

When death came, the family gathered to comfort the survivors. The common practice was for the family of the spouse of the deceased to come and take care of the body and prepare it for cremation. Young men of the opposite side from the deceased stood guard over the body while it was on display in the winter house. Others prepared for the cremation which usually took place on the fourth day after death. After the body had been burned, the bones were gathered and placed in a wooden box. Later, the box was placed in a hollowed out part of a tree or a totem pole known as a mortuary pole. Traditionally, all Tlingit were cremated except the shamans; their bodies were placed in a prominent place away from the village.

The death of an important person, such as a house spokesman, left a social vacuum. Each household needed a leader, and so a replacement had to be installed very soon. In most cases, the living spokesman selected one of his nephews to be his successor. If the spokesman failed to designate someone, the family had to make the decision. Again, women had an important voice in the choice of a successor. As soon as the heir had assembled enough gifts and food, he announced a memorial feast. Members of clans of the opposite side, usually those who had intermarried with the family, were invited to the feast. This celebration usually took place about a year after the death of the previous spokesman. The Tlingit term for this feast can be literally translated as "being invited." Messengers were sent through the villages, inviting people to attend. Today, the term "potlatch" is sometimes used to describe this feast. This term really comes from the Chinook jargon on the Columbia River. Farther south on the Northwest Coast, "potlatches" became competitive, and property was destroyed to demonstrate the family's wealth. Among the Tlingit, the feast always remained a memorial for the dead.

At the memorial, the new spokesman stepped out in front of the hosts and guests and announced that he was now the new representative of the house. Gifts were then given to the members of the opposite clans for the services they had provided at the time of death. Today, Tlingit sometimes refer to this memorial feast as "pay-off party" because people still help out with funeral expenses and they are repaid at this time. By attending the memorial, both the hosts and guests acknowledged the prerogatives of the new spokesman and his family. Among the Tlingit, a person could not buy his way into the position of spokesman; he had to be born to the right family. The memorial was simply a validation of his rights as successor. One of the most important parts of the memorial was a series of speeches given by the guests to which the hosts responded. Through a highly stylized format, the speakers comforted the hosts, using an intricate series of metaphors and comparisons.

The memorial was also a time for paying off any old debts and for several other social activities. It provided an opportunity to announce new family names. At this ceremony, an individual was brought out and set on a pile of gifts. His or her new name was publicly announced four times; each time the audience repeated the name. After the announcement, the gifts were distributed in honor of the newly named person. The giving of gifts to the guests placed them f in debt to the person just named. By accepting the presents, they now had to include that person in all social events and any payments or gifts given to the family or clan..

5. (Photo courtesy of Alaska State Library, V. Soboleff Collection, PCA 1-33) Tlingit dancers gathered for an historic celebration, wearing modern clothing as well as traditional garments such as Chilkat dancing robes.

In historic times, an intermediate memorial has been introduced; this is now called the "Forty Day Party." It seems to have started during the Russian period. At this event, there is usually a dinner, speeches, and eulogies somewhat like the traditional memorial. In most cases, church choirs from various denominations sing hymns. The atmosphere is one of a social-religious gathering, and there is no repayment for funeral services such as is done at the pay-off party.

It is sometimes difficult for modern Americans to appreciate the importance of the family in traditional Tlingit life. We have become so diversified that production, education, protection, banking, religion, law, and politics are now provided by outsiders or non-relatives. For the old Tlingit, the family provided all of these services for the individual. When asked what it meant to be Tlingit, Walter Williams once replied, "It means that you are never alone--in bad times or in good!"

TRADE AND WARFARE

There was extensive trade among all the inhabitants of the Northwest Coast. The Tlingit traveled along the coast and far inland. Many times their artifacts have been found among many other groups as trade goods or booty and had become treasured heirlooms among their new owners. Tlingit also possessed artifacts from other people. Some of the most important trading took place with the Athabascan people of interior Alaska and Canada. Routes to the interior were owned by specific family groups. A few of these were known as "grease trails" because one of the more valuable trade goods from the coast was eulachon oil. The trade with the interior people seems to have its origin in the ancient past; it may be that there has always been this type of exchange between coastal and interior people. In any case, the trade increased greatly during the fur trade of the eighteenth and nineteenth centuries. When the sea otter had been nearly exterminated, the Tlingit went inland to trade for other furs such as marten, fox, lynx and beaver.

Like the Tlingit, the interior Athabaskans traced their ancestry through the mother's side. In some instances, Tlingit families married their daughters to inland men and in this way, formed extensive trade alliances. The Chilkat Tlingit considered the interior to be their domain. The Hudson's Bay Company built a trading post 200 miles inland and named it Fort Selkirk. In 1852, the Chilkat destroyed it, claiming that the Company had trespassed on their territory. The coastal people dominated the interior people, especially when it came to exchanges. For instance, after buying European goods with furs, the Tlingit packed the items over the mountains to the Athabaskans. Here they demanded four to five times the amount of fur they had originally paid for the guns, knives, metal pots, traps, and other things. It is not surprising that in a very short time, many Tlingit families became wealthy and were able to sponsor great memorials and celebrations.

Among some Athabaskan speaking people, the term for a friend or "buddy " is *Gunaah*, and the Tlingit often refer to these neighbors as "Guna.naa." In addition to furs, the Tlingit often obtained Athabaskan songs and many of these songs are still sung today at Tlingit celebrations.

In addition to trading expeditions, the Tlingit raided other groups to capture slaves and to take revenge on enemies. Some of the battles were between Tlingit of different kwáans. At other times, they attacked the Haida, Tsimshian and Eskimos. A large raiding party might consist of five or six war canoes and sixty or eighty men. From childhood, a young Tlingit boy was taught that death in war brought honor to the family. The actual battles were oftentimes simply an ambush or minor skirmish. When they raided a village, the ideal time to attack was at daybreak while the enemy was still sleeping. An old Tlingit adage said that people should be up before the first raven call of the morning since that was when raiders might be lurking in the woods. Villages were located so that they would not be taken by surprise and the men were always cautious when they saw a canoe approaching. While out berry picking, women made noise to keep the bears away but were warned never to use a person's name. They were afraid that an enemy might lure her away by calling her by name as if they were a friend.

Intra-Tlingit battles have been long remembered among the families of those involved. One of the worst tragedies was when a group of Tlingit from one kwáan traveled to another settlement, apparently to carry out a deer ceremony and establish peace. When the guests were all inside the house, the hosts pulled out their knives and killed them. This treachery caused such a rift between the groups that it was only in historic times that a peace treaty was actually signed between both sides. One of the few benefits of Americanization was that the military stopped the warfare along the Northwest Coast.

Intellectual Culture

Although much of their religion was similar to that of other Northwest Coast cultures, some beliefs and practices were unique to the Tlingit. The basic assumption was that in addition to the physical world, there was another world of spirits. Both worlds or realities were important, but for success, it was necessary to be on good terms with the spirits. They had a belief in a "spirit above all other spirits" known as "haa kee naa yegi." The more modern term--probably due to Christian influence--is "Dei kee aan kaawoo," or "the far up chief," in reference to God the Father. The people felt a close relationship to their environment and the animals whom they considered to be like humans. In fact, it was believed that people could be transformed into animals and animals could take on human form. The underlying concept was that humans and animals both had immortal spirits. Death was simply a separation of the spirit from the body or container of the soul. It was all right to kill an animal, as long as it was treated respectfully because its spirit was set free to be born again in a new body. Belief in human reincarnation was based on the same principle; that is, when a person died, his or her spirit might return in a newborn infant.

One of the major celebrations farther south along the coast was the "First Salmon Ceremony." When the first salmon of the season was caught, it was given special care. Everyone shared in eating the flesh of the fish, but its bones were returned to the stream so that it would reborn. Among the Tlingit, this ceremony appears to have been less important, yet even in present times, there is sometimes a family dinner to celebrate the taking of the first salmon.

A careful study of the old stories indicates that they considered animals to be similar to humans in many ways. For example, the salmon are pictured as living just like humans only underwater in the nearby ocean. They dwelt in large clan houses for most of the year, walking around and talking like human beings. When they started up the streams to visit the woman at the head of the creeks, they donned their salmon bodies. While swimming up the stream, they were caught by humans and their spirits returned to the ocean to be born again.

Spirits were also feared. For instance, the land otter or "kush daa" were able to change into human form and come to the aid of a person. The rescued person became a land otter or "kush daa kaa"-- land otter person. It was also considered wrong to kill certain creatures, such as frogs or toads, because the person doing so would have bad luck.

Part of the belief was that spirits were able to communicate with each other. For instance, if a seal were killed improperly, or not handled with respect, the spirit of that seal told other seal spirits, and in the future, the animals avoided the offending party. Religious practices and prohibitions were oftentimes linked to success or failure in hunting, fishing, war, and other affairs. Religion was not an isolated, intellectual belief; it entered into nearly every aspect of daily life and shaped a person's destiny.

Spirits influenced a person's health. It was believed sickness might be caused by a foreign object getting into the body. The object had to be removed to bring about a cure. A person could also become sick when his or her spirit went wandering and failed to return to the body. Sometimes, spirits or souls traveled while the body slept. In these travels, or dreams, the soul visited far away places, met other spirits or even learned of future events. Everyone dreams and communicates with the spirit world. There were some people, however, who were specialists at dealing with spirits. These individuals were the "Ixt'." Missionaries and others called them "medicine men," "witches," or "sorcerers." The term that anthropologists use for such individuals, wherever they are found, is "shaman." The word was originally used by the Tungus of Siberia for their faith healers. According to accounts, Tlingit shamans were able to do marvelous things. They traveled under the sea to visit the spirits or flew thousands of miles to fight other shamans. They cured the sick by removing objects or returning wandering spirits to their bodies. Such a person was both respected and feared because of the great powers they were thought to possess.

It was said that some people invoked evil spirits. These individuals were considered witches. When an illness spread through a village or strange things happened, someone might be accused of witchcraft. If charged, a person could avoid punishment by confessing to the crime and promising to stop his or her evil practices. If the shaman claimed that a person was a witch and the accused refused to admit it or repent, the person was killed.

Little has been recorded concerning the old beliefs about life after death. There was a feeling that people should be cremated to insure a happy future life. It was important to recover the body of a drowned person so that it, too, could be burned. If a person had been killed, and the death not avenged, his spirit was said to wander among the clouds until the score had been evened.

MYTHS, LEGENDS AND STORIES

Among the Tlingit, the term "story" could have a range of meanings. It might refer to a creation myth, a legendary event in the past, or someone's personal experiences. Some stories are religious, and others are accounts of historical events. The famous Raven Stories describe the time of creation and are really quite humorous.

There are stories that were meant to educate the young people. For example, a long, action-packed legend is that of "Black Skin" or the "Strong Man." Here is the plot. A young man has black skin from sleeping near the fire. Everyone, except his aunt, is rude to him and ridicules him for his dark color while other young men refuse to work with him. What people do not know is that at night, as others are sleeping, he goes into the forest to build his strength. One night he wrestles with the spirit "Strength," and wins, thereby becoming the strongest man in the world. He keeps his power a secret from other villagers. The climax of the story comes when he is reluctantly allowed to share in a seal lion hunt. His uncle is killed by a sea lion. "Strong Man" runs through the canoe, smashing the rowers' seats as he does so. On land, he seizes the sea lion and tears it in half. The other hunters now realize how strong he is and fear that he will take revenge on them for the way they have treated him. They paddle away, leaving him stranded on the island. Eventually, he makes his way home but does not take revenge; he is a kind and gentle man.

There are lessons to be learned here. For example, a person should train and discipline himself to be ready for any encounter; never make fun of others because they may be stronger than one thinks; be careful what you say about people based on appearances. Tlingit oral literature is filled with many similar tales of adventure. Even today, they are still carry important messages.

TLINGIT ART

In the Tlingit culture, art was pervasive. House fronts, screens, corner posts and totem poles; ceremonial staffs, hats and blankets; cooking, storage and eating utensils; weapons, paddles and canoes; clothing and ornaments--everything was enhanced with exquisite art work. A person grew up surrounded and influenced by some of the finest art on the Northwest Coast. The environment, resources, and social and intellectual life are all reflected in Tlingit art. To fully appreciate this art, one must see it in its total cultural setting. Much of the art has a social role and is directly related to clan crests, history and legends. Tlingit were very protective of their rights to tell clan stories because with the authority to tell the story went the right to use the crest. Totem poles and other works of art cannot be "read" like a book. One must first know the history or legend, and with that information, one is then able to understand the meaning of the art. The illustration of totem poles provided by Goldbelt Corporation, (the Juneau Native corporation formed following the Alaska Native Claims Settlement Act, Figure I) shows the relationship of the figures to the oral narratives.

Nearly all of the designs were of animals but some others were based upon mythical creatures, such as Thunderbird, while others represented geographic features, for instance, a mountain. In the old art, there were no floral designs. It was only after contact and trade that flowers began to appear on vests, blankets, and other clothing.

Tlingit art, like other Northwest Coast art, reflects a certain sense of humor by playing tricks with art. For example, at first glance it may appear that opposite sides of a bentwood box are the same. But after careful inspection, it turns out that each side of the box is different. A bowl or rattle may have several different interpretations, depending on how it is held. One has to look at some items very carefully to figure out exactly what the artist has done (Photo 2).

The Tlingit used a few special techniques, particularly in reducing three-dimensional figures to two dimensions for example, with screens and boxes. One practice was to portray a creature as split in half, leaving it joined only at the head. For instance, a shark might be shown as split from the tail to the head with the head portrayed as the central unit. The rest of the body folded symmetrically along the sides. Another technique was to present an x-ray view of the creature by showing the ribs or representing joints by the use of ovoids. In many cases, the artist avoided leaving any blank areas such as on screens or in the Chilkat blankets; every bit of space was filled (Photo 3).

The Tlingit generally used three colors as supplements to their carving. Black was used to outline the basic design, known as the formline. This continuous line flowed from one part of the work to the next, uniting it into integrated unit. The second color red, was used for secondary designs and accents. Secondary parts were usually enclosed within the primary black formline. A third color, blue or blue-green, was painted in where the wood had been cut away. If a box or screen had not been carved, the designs could be simply painted on the surface.

The Tlingit artist worked under many cultural restraints. He had to be careful in the way he depicted the stories and legends so as not to give offense. Second, he had to follow the traditional forms for hands, feet, faces, fins, wings, paws and general animal forms. Third, he had to adapt the designs to the material and space available whether it be a totem pole, box, or any other work of art. Finally, there may have been time constraints when objects were needed quickly for a ceremonial occasion. In spite of these constraints, each artist expressed his individuality. Some men became famous artists, and even slaves with artistic ability were given special treatment.

Women had their own arts. As mentioned earlier, they were known for their Chilkat blankets and tunics. Most of these blankets were woven in symmetrical patterns, but some early European sketches, show robes with free-flowing designs. A predecessor to the Chilkat blanket was made of squares and is known as a "Raven's Tail" blanket. Only a few old examples of this type of blanket are found in museums, but in recent times, some women have revived this style of weaving.

The Tlingit were also highly skilled basket weavers, making both spruce root and cedar bark baskets in a variety of shapes and sizes. Cooking baskets were so tightly woven that they were used to carry water. Other baskets were used for berry picking, storing and carrying food or a variety of other everyday needs. The finer baskets have precise geometric designs woven into them through a form of surface embroidery. The various patterns have traditional names and usually appear in three bands.

6. (Photo courtesy Alaska State Library, Case and Draper Collection, PCA 39-197) A collection of woven baskets, containers and covered utensils for sale to visitors to Southeastern Alaska.

Spruce roots were also used to weave both ceremonial and everyday hats. Many of these hats, and some baskets have traditional crest designs painted on them, and some hats have "potlatch rings" on the top, indicating the owner's status.

Tlingit also had performing arts such as songs and dances. They were one of the few Indian societies in North America to use a form of harmony in their singing. They had songs for love and war, for mourning and joy, as well as to tell stories or simply entertain. During ceremonials, such as those for the dead, hour after hour was spent singing and dancing. Members of one side often competed with their counterparts in song and dance. It was also considered prestigious to use songs taken from other people. They were considered valuable property taken from others. Many of the opening songs at Tlingit ceremonials were from the Athabaskans of the interior.

Unlike paintings and carvings, if a song or dance is not performed every generation, it is lost to future generations. In the past, the use of the Tlingit language and ceremonies was ridiculed and prohibited by teachers and missionaries. Because of this pressure, many songs and dances have disappeared. Today, there is an attempt to videotape and record the elders' performances in order to preserve the music and dance for future generations.

A final art form was storytelling. We cannot know for sure what it was like two hundred years ago to hear a Tlingit orator. However, the few elderly people who still recite the old stories do so with great skill. The late Walter Williams was a famous Tlingit orator. On his visits to elementary schools, children sat around him, totally enraptured with his presence as he told stories, sang and danced. He acted out each scene. Listeners--even adults--were completely enthralled with his presentations. Even while explaining Tlingit life to academicians, he many times had them hanging on his every word. Those who had the opportunity to see him got an idea of what it must have been like to hear an old Tlingit storyteller.

The Spanish explorers expressed regret that they were not able to learn about the Tlingit's beliefs, religion, or philosophy. Most other Europeans, with a few exceptions such as the saintly Father Veniaminov, were not interested in what they considered an inferior or savage way of thinking. As a result, little has been recorded of

Tlingit values, attitudes, and intellectual culture at the time of contact. It is only in the oral narratives and old stories that we find some of the beliefs and ideals of the Tlingit prior to contact. As with the songs and dances, there is a concerted effort to record the elderly who are still able to express and explain some of the more abstract aspects of their culture.

FIGURE 1

Naatslanei was a great hunter and respected in his village

Naatslanei liked to hunt and fish with his three brothers in law.

The three brothers were jealous of Naatslanei and left him on a reef at low tide to drown when the tide covered the reef

The youngest brother did'nt want to leave him, but he couldn't help.

A loon appeared and took Naatslanei to a secret world inside the reef

Here were people like him who put him in a bubble and he drifted to shore

Naatslanei's wife was contacted and told to bring his tools to him secretly

He carved a mean looking monster which he called "Keet".

The first one did not swim - but after carving the second one of yellow cedar, it began to swim.

"I have created you to avenge a wrong - doing. Three men will be in a canoe. Dispose of the two bad ones but don't harm the young-est."

The killerwhale eliminated the two brothers and swam the youngest back to shore.

Naatslanei then ordered the killer whale to never harm man again and let Keet go.

CREATION OF KILLERWHALE

Eagle and Raven representing the Tlingt Nation.

Woman - representing a matrilinial society

The maternal uncle is responsible for the training of his nephews.

Ixt' (medicine man) foretells the future and can call upon powerful spirits to heal sickness.

Kooshdaa Kaa (landotter)

Owl woman - while harvesting herring one day near Sitka her family mistreated her. She went into the woods and became an owl.

Loo ko náo, the demon, moved like the wind and awoke from trances in strange places.

Tux gwas', a wildman, wanders in the woods with an adze, when you see his spiral cuts in a tree and fast - you will become wealthy.

Lá noo xee do kw (Auke woman) a woman and baby survived an attack on the village.

LEGENDS AND BELIEFS

Bear - strongman's clan

A huge sealion killed a hunter of the village.

The uncles, seeking revenge, met to organize a plan. All the nephews went into training to avenge the dead hunter. In the winter the young men would bathe in the salt water and be whipped with branches to keep the blood circulating. One nephew, who did not train with the others and was thought to be lazy, liked to sleep close to the fire. His skin became dark and he was named Duk t'ootl. He trained secretly at night and when the day of the contest came he was ready. The young boys would attempt to kill the sealion bare-handed.

Duk t'ootl had to beg to go because everyone made fun of him.

After all of the young men had failed to kill the large sealion Duk t'ootl grabbed the sealion and ripped it in half on the reef.

STRONGMAN

(Illustration courtesy Goldbelt Corporation, Juneau, Alaska)

64

Chilkat dancing robe or blanket, with the "diving whale" design. (Alaska State Museum. Item # II-B-1841. Photo by Steve Henrickson)

Carved rattle in form of a bird with a man and frog on its back, connected by a tongue. Reportedly carved in Sitka at the time of the massacre, 1802. (Alaska State Museum. Item # II-B-66. Photo by Steve Henrickson)

History and Change

RAVEN'S STRANGE VISITORS

It was a warm summer day as old Yeil-ḵaa sat carving in front of his family's house. Suddenly the wolf call, the warning signal, was heard across the village. "Raven is coming! Raven is coming!" the young warrior cried out as people rushed to the beach. "I saw Raven, but he has white wings and is moving from side to side on the water." Everyone ran to the point of land to see the legendary Raven. Yeil-ḵaa came tottering behind the others. Although he was old in body, his mind was still quick and strong. He thought to himself, "Raven was white before he was stuck in Petrel's smoke hole. Did he change his color again?"

A harsh, grating sound was heard, and Raven folded his white wings, sitting on the water far from the shore. Yeil-ḵaa could sense fear among the people. He knew he had to show courage. "I am Yeil-ḵaa, Raven Man," he said, "and I will go to meet Raven. I will ask him to treat us kindly."

The people helped the old man into his small hunting canoe and pushed him out towards Raven, still sitting on the water. As he got close, Raven appeared to be made of wood. Strange looking people were walking around on Raven. Yeil-ḵaa stood up in his canoe, spread his arms in the traditional sign of peace, and said, "Raven, have mercy on us poor ones."

A woven line was dropped down and hanging on to it, Yeil-ḵaa was lifted up. Stepping on to Raven, he realized that this was a large canoe, larger than anyone had ever seen. This was not Raven. These were funny-looking people with light hair and blue eyes. Their speech was unlike any he had ever heard.

Yeil-ḵaa was now afraid that these strangers had lost their minds and had been sent away from their people. They offered him pieces of something hard and white that looked like part of a human skull, but he refused lest he become a witch like them. They then set before him a bowl filled with what appeared to be warm, white worms, much like the maggots one finds on rotten fish. Some men were putting spoonfuls of whatever this was into their mouths. Finally, someone handed him a small container of a strange-smelling liquid; it was red like blood. The stranger took his cup of liquid, lifted it up high, and then drank it, with signs indicating that Yeil-ḵaa should do the same. The old man would not drink blood.

65

The one who seemed to be the leader, grabbed Yeil-kaa's otter skin cap, while handing him a large piece of metal, shaped like a bowl. When the stranger struck it with a metal rod, the bowl made a loud, ringing sound. He presented the bowl to Yeil-kaa who turned it carefully in his hands. This was not like the metal he had seen before; this was yellow. Another man took Yeil-kaa's otter skin clothes, while holding out a bar of metal in the other hand, indicating he wished to trade. Yeil-kaa slipped off his robe and seized the metal. He now had two pieces of metal from these demented wanderers. Carefully, he pointed to his canoe while clutching his treasures in his other arm. Taking a rope with a loop on the end, they placed it around him. Slowly he was lowered into his canoe. He quickly paddled to shore.

Back at the village, he told everyone, "It is not Raven. It is a large canoe of strange men, made crazy by drifting on the ocean. They are eating skulls and worms and drinking blood. If they come ashore, we will have to kill them."

Later that day, while the people of the village watched from shore, six of these strangers paddled around the bay in a small boat. Early the next morning, the visitors raised the large white skins, and the wind blew them away.

[Until his death a few years later, Yeil-kaa told and retold the story of this encounter with these creatures on their huge canoe. Later, when more of these vessels were seen, his descendants knew that he had been the first to meet the Whitemen and that they had offered him biscuits, rice and red rum. They have kept his story down to the present time.]

(Adapted from the Tlingit account of the arrival of La Perouse at Lituya Bay in 1786.)

THE EARLY YEARS OF TRADE

The first recorded meeting of Tlingit and Whitemen occurred on July 15, 1741. On that day, Alexei Chirikov, aboard the vessel *Saint Paul*, sighted land at a latitude of about 55 degrees, 21 minutes north. He sent one of his boats for fresh water, but it did not come back. He waited offshore, and later dispatched a second boat with instructions to bring both boats back immediately. They failed to return. The next morning, two Indian canoes came out, but upon seeing the ship, they returned to shore without meeting Chirikov. He had no other boat to send and so reluctantly left the area to begin his return voyage to Kamchatka.

The actual fate of Chrikov's men remains a mystery, however the Tlingit do have a story of two boatloads of men who came ashore to get water and decided not to return to their ship. The story goes on to say that they eventually married into the Tlingit people and settled at Klawock. The story may be related to the fate of Chirikov's men.

SPANISH EXPLORATIONS

The Spanish were the next Europeans to reach Southeastern Alaska. In 1774, Juan Perez was ordered to explore the west coast of North America as far north as latitude 60 degrees. He sailed from New Spain to the coast of Prince of Wales Island, but a storm forced him to turn back without going ashore in what is today Alaska. The following year, Bruno Heceta and Perez traveled north aboard the *Santiago*, accompanied by the *Sonora*, commanded by Juan Francisco de Bodega y Quadra. *The Santiago* turned back, but the *Sonora* finally anchored first near Sitka, then discovered a large inlet which they named Bucareli Entrance.

In 1779, Don Ignacio de Arteaga y Bazan aboard the *Princesa*, and Don Juan Francisco de la Bodega y Quadra in charge of the *Favorita* returned to Bucareli Entrance. For two weeks they explored the adjacent bays, inlets, and harbors, naming each of them. They continued on north where they explored Valdez Arm, Prince William Sound, Cook Inlet, and Kodiak Island

Besides charting the areas visited, the Spanish described the Indians. The reports from these expedition are some of the earliest and best descriptions we have of the Tlingit and Haida of southern Alaska. This area--Bucareli Bay, San Alberto Bay and the Gulf of Esquibel--was the border between the Tlingit and Haida. Today, Tlingit and Haida live at Bucareli Bay in the villages of Craig and Klawock.

The Europeans were surprised that the Indian's knew about iron and sought it in trade. The sailors had to be on guard since the Indians tried to steal any metal objects they could. The purpose of the Spanish explorations was to determine the extent of Russian occupation, and to see if there were lands which might be claimed for the Spanish throne. The Spaniards had been instructed to make friendly contact with the Indians and not to attack or offend them. From later reports by the British explorers Portlock and Dixon, it appears that the Spanish unknowingly started a smallpox epidemic. The disease may have spread across all of Southeastern, infecting even the Indians of interior Alaska and Canada. If this smallpox epidemic was as deadly as those reported later in historical times, a major portion of the Native population may have died in the next few years.

Since they had not found any Russians in the area, the Spanish made no further explorations in this area for the next four years. In 1779, another expedition set out under the command of Don Ignacio de Arteaga y Bazan aboard the *Princesa*, and Don Juan Francisco de la Bodega y Quadra in charge of the *Favorita*. They returned to Bucareli Bay and later proceeded north where they explored Valdez Arm, Prince William Sound, Cook Inlet, and Kodiak Island.

There was a fourth expedition in 1788 under the command of Esteban Jose Martinez, and Gonzalo Lopez de Haro as second in command. There were subsequent voyages to Alaska in 1790 and 1791 under Salvador Fidalgo and Francisco de Eliza. Their assignment again was to evaluate the Russian power in the region.

The next major Spanish explorer to Southeastern was Admiral Alejandro Malaspina aboard the *Descubierta* accompanied by Jose Bustamente as captain of the *Atrevida*. The ships anchored in Port Mulgrave, today the site of the village of Yakutat. Here they spent more than two weeks exploring the area, gathering scientific information and meeting with the Indians. This was the most complete scientific expedition to Southeastern up to this time.

In 1792, Don Jacinto Caamano undertook the final Spanish voyage of exploration to Alaska. He returned to Bucareli Bay, explored nearby areas and eventually compiled navigation charts for the region.

Outside of smallpox epidemic, the Spanish had little impact on the Native people. Their greatest contribution was their descriptions of the people along with their technology, housing, and customs. The artifacts they collected are now preserved in the Museo de America in Madrid while their charts are housed at the Museo Naval. Even though several of the Spanish documents have been translated into English, many other journals, log books and correspondence which contain important information regarding the Tlingit, remain untranslated

EARLY FUR TRADERS

Soon after the first Russians colonized the Aleutian Islands, other fur traders discovered that Alaska was a rich source of sea otter, whose pelts brought a high price on the Chinese market. The first traders on the Northwest Coast were British. By 1786, of the eight vessels on the coast, several were cruising Alaskan waters. Two of the British captains, Nathaniel Portlock and George Dixon, kept accurate logs which include descriptions of the Tlingit at Yakutat and Sitka.

By 1792, there were thirty trading ships on the coast, but now the list included several American, French, and Portuguese vessels. Before long, the "Boston Men," as the Americans came to be called, assumed the leadership in the fur trade. American and British traders had an important advantage over the Russians. By treaty, the only place in China where the Russians were allowed to trade their furs was at the inland city of Kyakhta. The alternative was to carry the furs across Siberia to the Russian market. It usually took more than a year to transport the furs from Sitka to Kyakhta. American and British traders, on the other hand, were allowed to trade directly with the Chinese at Hong Kong or Canton. Coming from Europe or New England, the ships carried a cargo of trade goods. After a summer of exchange on the Northwest Coast, the ships took the furs directly to China. Here they traded for Chinese goods and returned to the North American coast for a second season. Some ships returned to the Northwest Coast year after year. It has been estimated that in one or two years of successful trading, the owners of a ship were able to recover the entire cost of the vessel and its cargo and still make a sizeable profit.

The Russians were handicapped by the fact that they had no settlement in Southeastern until the late 1790's. By that time, the Tlingit were accustomed to the high prices and trade goods carried by the Americans and British ships. Since the vessels were here only in the summer and constantly moving about, the traders were willing to exchange firearms and liquor for the Natives' furs. The Russians, on the other hand hoping to establish settlements in Alaska, and did not want to put firearms in the hands of the Indians, especially those of the belligerent Tlingit.

Only a few of these early traders left any record or descriptions of the people. Their whole purpose was to get the furs, make a fortune and to keep their trade routes secret. A few English traders met the British military ships and assisted them. Of course, relationships with the Indians were not always friendly. Several times there were skirmishes in which both Europeans and Indians were killed.

The principal changes in the daily life of the Tlingit and Haida came about through the introduction of new tools and technology. For instance, by 1800, there were thousands of totem poles on the Northwest Coast where previously only a few had been reported. The advances in carving and woodworking were probably sparked by the abundance of metal tools. One of the most popular trade items in the early days were "toes"--small strips of iron or steel that could be fashioned into a variety of tools such as adzes and knives. As early as the 1790's, some captains were complaining that the market for iron tools had been flooded and that the Indians demanded more elaborate goods. Soon, Chinese storage trunks stood side by side with bentwood boxes in Tlingit homes. Chinese coins were commonplace on the coast. In the Field Museum in Chicago, there is an interesting vest, completely covered with these coins; it was probably used as a coat of armor. Tlingit had easy access to pots, pans, knives, mirrors, spy glasses, and several kinds of firearms. European clothing began to replace traditional bark and skin dress. Some lineages and their leaders became wealthy and powerful, enabling them to sponsor elaborate feasts and memorials and to equip raiding parties with the latest weapons.

It seems that for the most part, the social and intellectual culture of the Tlingit went unchanged throughout most of this time. They continued to be the masters of their homelands, tolerating the traders as long as they did not interfere with the aboriginal power structure or try to build a permanent settlement. This arrangement changed with the coming of the Russians and even more so after the purchase of Alaska by the United States.

BRITISH EXPLORERS

The British had several motives for exploring the Northwest Coast. One of their goals was to assess the extent to which they might lay claim to the western coast of the continent. They kept probing the shoreline to estimate the Russian presence. Secondly, they also wanted to profit from the fur trade, and finally, they tried to find the legendary Northwest Passage across North America. If this reported waterway did exist, they would no longer have to go around Africa or South America to reach their colonial outposts. Several writers had said that they sailed from the Northwest Coast to Hudson Bay. The British plan was to examine every inlet on the northern coast that led either north or east and to see if one might be the entrance to this legendary waterway. As it turned out, of course, the only real Northwest Passage is through the northern ice fields at the top of the continent. But in the eighteenth century, geographers knew nothing about this part of the world.

In July of 1776, Captain James Cook began a voyage to the Northwest Coast, hoping to discover the Northwest Passage and thereby win a large reward. Although he sailed along the coast of Southeastern Alaska in 1778, he did not examine any of the inside waters. He did, however, rename the mountain which the Spaniards had called Mount Jacinto; he called it Mount Edgecumbe. Eight years later, Captain John Meares, a former Navy Lieutenant turned trader and adventurer, explored and charted parts of Southeastern Alaska. Later, Meares was involved in a dispute with the Spanish over the control of Nootka Sound on Vancouver Island. A settlement was achieved with the signing of the Nootka Sound Convention in Madrid in 1790.

George Vancouver served as a midshipman under Cook on the *Discovery*. In 1790 he was asked to lead a new expedition to the Northwest Coast to conclude the Nootka agreement and to complete a comprehensive search for the Northwest Passage. Among his officers were Peter Puget, Joseph Baker, Joseph Whidbey and James Johnstone. Their names were later given to many geographic features on the Northwest Coast. Vancouver began his survey of the coast along what is today northern California. By 1793, he had examined the coast as far north as Portland Canal, which today separates Alaska from British Columbia. In the summer of that year, he and his crew carefully surveyed and charted every inlet they could find leading north or east. They retained the Spanish place names already on the charts, but gave new names to hundreds of other features. To this day, a vast number of place names in Southeastern come from Vancouver's survey. By the end of the 1793 season, they had searched the southern half of Southeastern Alaska. After clearing the northern end of Prince of Wales Island, they turned south to California, traveling on to Hawaii for the winter.

In March of 1794, the two ships, the *Discovery* and *Chatham* set out for Alaska. After separating at sea, they rejoined in Cook Inlet. Completing their survey around Kodiak Island and the Kenai peninsula, the vessels returned to Southeastern Alaska. At Yakutat, an estimated 1,000 Kodiak natives were seen hunting sea otter under Russian supervision. By this time, Vancouver's health was failing, so that the actual boat surveys were carried out by Whidbey and Johnstone. Three boats surveyed the northern end of Southeastern Alaska and returned to the *Discovery* which then sailed along the outside coast to the point where they had finished their survey the previous year. They continued to study every inlet on the eastern shore up to the site of present day Juneau. It was here that they realized that there was no Northwest Passage.

Vancouver was an extremely careful navigator and surveyor. As a result, his charts, published in 1798, enabled traders and explorers to expand their operations in these waters. Vancouver's work was so accurate that even Russian map makers merely added minor details to his charts. Nearly all of the more than 300 Alaskan place names given by Vancouver, remain in use today. The Americans, particularly New England traders, increased their activities on the Northwest Coast. By 1814, there were only three British trading vessels working the coast. There were hardly any Russian ships in the area until a new settlement was begun at Sitka in 1799.

RUSSIAN PRESENCE IN SOUTHEASTERN

After consolidating control over the southwestern coast of Alaska, Alexander Baranov, the manager of the Shelikov Company, decided to expand into the Alaskan panhandle. The first attempt at settlement was at Yakutat in 1795. The following year a second group was sent there, and it remained a Russian settlement until it was destroyed by the Tlingit in 1805. Farther south, at Sitka, the fort which the Russians had built in 1799, was destroyed by the Tlingit in 1802. The Russians recaptured Sitka in 1804 and made it the headquarters of the Russian American Company until 1867. The only other permanent European settlement in this region was Fort Dionysius, built by the Russians in 1835 at the present site of Wrangell. Later, it was turned over to the Hudson's Bay Company,

73

and renamed Fort Stikine. An indication of the variety of people coming to the Northwest Coast can be seen by the fact that of the 21 regular laborers at the fort, 19 were Hawaiian! The Hudson's Bay Company also had a small outpost at Taku Harbor, just south of Juneau. Fort Durham, as it was called, was in operation from 1840-1842.

Although Alaska has often been described as Russian America, until 1868, the Tlingit actually controlled nearly all of the territory. From the Native point of view, they tolerated the Russian presence at Sitka as a means of having access to trade goods. The Russians were well armed, but so were the Indians. The Europeans were always on guard whenever they left the stockade. As late as 1855, the Tlingit attacked the Sitka stockade.

The Russians brought about other changes in the Tlingit culture. When smallpox epidemics swept through region in 1836, the Sitka Indians who had been vaccinated were spared. The influence of the shaman was reduced since it was clear that he was not as effective as the Russian doctors. The missionaries were quick to take the lead, and through the efforts of men like the saintly Ivan Veniaminov, some Tlingit became Christians. According to the Church records, by 1843, at least 100 Tlingit had become members of the Orthodox Church. The Russians also provided education for some Tlingit and other Natives, as well as for those known as "creoles," the descendants of marriages between Russian and Natives. At Sitka, some Tlingit and creoles learned to read and write; a few became skilled at trades such as woodworking and shipbuilding.

Successive epidemics of measles and smallpox took their toll on the Native people. There is no way to determine exactly how many lives were lost due to these new diseases, but it appears that there was a great decline in population in the first half of the nineteenth century.

As was mentioned earlier, the drop in the number of sea otter pelts taken on the coast, prompted the Tlingit to increase their

7. (Photo courtesy of Alaska State Library, Early Prints, PCA 01-343)
Lincoln Street in Sitka after the purchase of Alaska by the United States.
St. Michael's Cathedral in center.

inland trade. This coastal-interior exchange continued until the purchase of Alaska, when the two groups were divided by the United States-Canadian boundary.

For the most part, the traditional Tlingit social system remained intact. There were some cases of marriage between Russian men and Indian women, but since ancestry was traced matrilineally, the children were still considered Tlingit. Today, some of the prominent Tlingit leaders are descendants of these creole families.

EARLY AMERICAN INFLUENCE IN SOUTHEASTERN

The Americanization of Alaska initiated a series of events which deeply affected Tlingit life and culture. For the first time, newcomers began to settle in the Tlingit territory. Because the settlers were supported by the government and the military, American laws were imposed and enforced. The traditional Tlingit laws were totally ignored, particularly in regard to their rules of ownership. The rationalization was that somehow the territory was a "wilderness" completely owned by the United States government. This total disregard for Tlingit law was necessary if the newcomers were to claim the land. If they had acknowledged Tlingit law, they would have had to purchase the land from the aboriginal owners; this the settlers refused to do. As a result, they simply seized Tlingit lands, creeks, and resources, pushing aside the Natives. The ethnocentric prejudice of the settlers is obvious in their descriptions of the Indians as "savages," "uncivilized barbarians." This way of thinking gave rise to discrimination and injustice. The Euroamericans justified their actions by claiming to be more civilized and therefore superior to the Tlingit. The missionaries and educators saw absolutely no value in the old culture and were determined to wipe away all traces of the traditional society, religion, and language. Throughout all of these forced changes, the Tlingit, like other American Indians, had little to say about the way they were treated. It was not until 1924 that they were declared citizens. By that time, their lands had been taken away, and their traditional society and culture disrupted. They were considered "wards" of the government, savage children who had no rights except those reluctantly granted by the newcomers.

EARLY MILITARY CONTROL

Sitka, the old Russian headquarters, became the capital of the new Territory. The first few years of occupation were disastrous. Carpetbaggers, drifters, soldiers, businessmen and others poured into Alaska, creating social chaos. In addition to the widespread drunkenness, prostitution, and corruption in Sitka, the Natives in the outlying areas also suffered. For example, in 1869, after two white men were killed by the Indians at Kake, the vessel *Saginaw* was sent to punish the offenders. Aware of the approaching ship, most of the Indians fled the village. General Davis then ordered his men to destroy the entire settlement. The same year, following fights between Tlingit and soldiers, the village at Fort Wrangell was also bombarded. In 1882, at the village of Angoon, an explosion killed two Indians and so the Tlingit took two white men as hostages until compensation was paid. In response to their demands, the Revenue cutter *Service* was dispatched to the site. They secured the release of the two men but again bombarded and destroyed the village as well. It was this "gunboat diplomacy" that forced the Tlingit to submit to the demands of the government.

In the meantime, missionaries had arrived and opened schools in Wrangell and Sitka. Sheldon Jackson first came to Alaska as a missionary and in 1885 was made the General Agent for Education in the Territory. What had started as the Sitka Industrial Training School eventually evolved into the Sheldon Jackson College, which still provides higher educational for Southeastern Alaska.

Another clergyman who had an important influence on Alaska Native history was the Reverend William Duncan. As an Anglican missionary, he wanted to isolate his followers from the evil influences of the Whitemen. In 1887, he brought his Tsimshian congregation from Canada to Annette Island in the new territory of Alaska. In 1891, Metlakatla, as it was called, became the only formal Indian reservation in all of Alaska.

Ten years after the purchase of Alaska, the Army was recalled from the Territory, and the Navy was given the job of maintaining law and order for the next seven years.

8. (Photo courtesy Alaska State Library, "A summer on the Thetis, 1898." PCA 27-5) View of the interior of a clan house.

THE RUSH FOR GOLD AND FISH

Following the gold rush to California, many prospectors began moving north. By 1880, they had worked their way to Alaska where they made several new discoveries. One of the major finds was near the present site of Juneau. By 1884, the miners demanded some kind of legal system to provide legal title for their claims. That same year, the first Organic Act was passed, making Alaska both a civil and judicial district. In that Act was a statement which said:

> Indians or other persons in said district shall not be disturbed in the possession of any lands actually in their

use or occupation or now claimed by them but the terms under which such persons may acquire title to such lands is reserved for future legislation by Congress.

It would be another eighty-seven years of historical change before that legislation would be forthcoming.

With the gold rush of the 1880's many new settlers arrived. They prospected not only the mainland but the islands as well. As the larger mines went into operation, they hired some Tlingit, but many of the workers, including some Chinese, were brought in from outside. Over the next 50 years, in addition to the gold there were copper, limestone and gypsum mines and a marble quarry in Southeastern.

9. (Photo courtesy of Alaska State Library, Early Prints, Tlingit Groups. PCA 01-1910) Group of Tlingit men in contemporary dress about 1910.

Meanwhile the miners took the minerals that the Tlingit had not used, and their lands as well. In 1906, a law was passed allowing the heads of Indian and Eskimo families to obtain title to 160 acres of non-mineral lands, but it was not until 1914 that any surveys were done. Another group was harvesting the salmon, the foundation of the traditional economy. The first canneries in

10. (Photo courtesy of Alaska State Library, Case and Draper Collection. PCA 39-252) Formal portrait of a woman wearing a Chilkat robe and tunic and entitled "Potlatcher."

Alaska were built at Klawock and Sitka in 1878. For several years there were also plants for rendering herring and whale oil. As a result of these new industries, Tlingit were crowded out of their own traditional lands by newcomers. Since Indians were not legally citizens, they had no way to protect their streams, berry patches, and village areas against the claims made by the new immigrants and companies.

By the late 1800's, canneries had begun to construct fish traps. At first the traps were permanently set in one place, but as time went on, these were replaced by floating traps that could be relocated from season to season. These traps were able to catch nearly every salmon headed to the spawning streams. The first traps were set at the mouths of streams, but before long this practice was outlawed. The expansion of fish traps took away the very basis of the Tlingit economy, but with no legal rights, reservations, or political power there was nothing they could do.

The final blow to the traditional lifeways came with the establishment of the Alexander Archipelago Forest Reserve in 1902. Five years later, the Reserve was transformed into the Tongass National Forest and included all lands not previously homesteaded or claimed by the miners and canneries. Now the Tlingit had lost all legal access to their streams and waterways and their lands

Seventy or eighty years later, it is hard for people to realize what effect all of these actions had on the Tlingit people. There was blatant discrimination and injustice. Newspapers described the Indians in such derogatory and insulting terms that today such statements would bring a flood of lawsuits for libel. In the southern portion of the Panhandle, the government wanted to consolidate the Haida people, and so the new village of Hydaburg was created and most of the older Haida villages were abandoned. Soon after the turn of the century, it seemed that the efforts to eliminate Tlingit society and culture would be successful. But the Tlingit and other Natives were beginning to make themselves heard. With formal education and innate ability, they took the initiative for citizenship and equality.

THE TLINGIT-HAIDA FIGHT FOR JUSTICE

The turning point in Tlingit history came with the formation of the Alaska Native Brotherhood in 1912 and the Alaska Native Sisterhood soon thereafter. Most of the founders were educated Natives who decided to fight for their civil rights. They accepted the fact that outsiders with their new culture were here to stay. Their constitution is a good example of how well they had learned their lessons. The first two articles state:

> "The purpose of this organization shall be to assist and encourage the Native in his advancement from his native state to his place among the cultivated races of the world, to oppose, discourage and overcome the narrow injustice of race and prejudice, and to aid in the development of the Territory to be worthy of a place among the States of North America."

> "Those eligible to membership shall be the English speaking members of the Native residents of the Territory of Alaska."

These statements are noteworthy for a couple of reasons. First, the stated goal is to overcome racial injustice and prejudice for the betterment of the Territory. The organization was not designed for cultural preservation. Apparently, the founders knew that without citizenship and equal rights, they would continue to suffer economically, socially and culturally. The immediate concern was for equal rights.

At first glance, the second article might seem to discourage the use of Tlingit or any Native language. The organizers felt that if the Indians and Eskimos of Alaska were to compete, they would have to learn the foreigners' language. They were not denouncing their own languages; they knew that they would have to speak English to obtain equality.

The first by-law of their constitution says that "Robert's Rules of Order shall be the authority on parliamentary law in both the grand and the subordinate camps." They wanted everyone to know that they understood the Whiteman's ways and would compete in proper parliamentary form. Over the years, the Alaska Native Brotherhood and Sisterhood have become famous for their skill in parliamentary procedure.

In 1915, the second Territorial Legislature passed an act enfranchising all Alaska Natives who could show proof of general qualification by having abandoned tribal ways and adopting a civilized way of life. Finally, on June 6, 1924, American Indians and Eskimos were declared citizens of the United States and entitled to vote. Sixty years after the Emancipation Proclamation, the descendants of the very first Americans were recognized as having a right to be here. But by that time, most of their lands had been taken away. They were outcasts in their homeland.

In 1924, William Paul, a Tlingit, became the first Alaska Native elected to the Territorial Legislature. Following his lead, several other Natives were elected to the Territorial Legislature. In 1948, Frank Peratrovitch of Klawock became the first Native to be elected President of the Territorial Senate. In addition to prejudice and discrimination towards Alaska Natives, there was actual segregation in many public places. In 1945, the Territorial Legislature finally passed an anti-discrimination law.

By the early 1930's, the ANB, as the Brotherhood had come to be known, began to represent fishermen in their negotiations with the canneries. The ANB was told that if it wanted to represent the fishermen, it would have to admit non-Natives into their membership, and so their constitution was revised to allow non-Natives to join.

The Indian Reorganization Act of 1934 (IRA) had two major impacts on the Indians of Southeastern Alaska. The Act allowed villages to establish a form of local government known as an IRA village council. Several of the smaller settlements adopted this form of government, and in the early 1980's the councils were seen as avenues for winning Native sovereignty.

11. (Photo courtesy Alaska State Library, Case and Draper Collection, PCA 39-408) Picture of the Native band from Klukwan, taken in Juneau in 1912.

Another provision in the Act permitted areas to be set aside as Native Reserves. These guaranteed the Indians some lands for their traditional hunting and fishing or for future development. These reserves should not be confused with the Indian reservations found in other states. The only true Indian reservation in Alaska is Metlakatla on Annette Island. This was originally Tlingit territory, but as was mentioned earlier, it was set aside for the Tsimshian immigrants who came with Father Duncan from Canada. Over the years, many people have compared this village with other Native villages in Alaska. But any such comparison would be inappropriate, since Metlakatla is a unique situation. For example, their roads, schooling and other facilities are provided by the federal government. During World War II, the military maintained a large airfield on the island, and later it became the airport for Ketchikan. Since the airport was located in an Indian Reservation, the Indians were able to charge rent on the lands used by the military. Again, after fish traps were outlawed by the State of Alaska, the people of Metlakatla were allowed to keep their traps since State law does not apply to Indian reservations. And so the reservation has had many advantages that other villages have not had.

After achieving citizenship, the next step for the Native people was to seek compensation for the lands taken by the creation of the Tongass National Forest. The Tlingit-Haida Jurisdictional Act of 1935 gave the Indians the authority to sue the government for compensation. The Alaska Native Brotherhood and Sisterhood had paid most of the costs for the legal expertise needed to pursue the claims. But then they were told that since they had non-Native members, a new organization would have to be formed to carry out the suit. This new group became the Central Council of the Tlingit-Haida. With the onset of World War II, little was done with the lawsuit. But soon after the war, the Indian Claims Commission was established to settle these types of disputes. The Tlingit-Haida had originally hoped to receive about $80,000,000 as compensation, but the Commission awarded them only $7,546,053--less than 10% of what they were asking.

Since the settlement, the Central Council of Tlingit-Haida, has been formally recognized as a "tribe" and contracts with the Bureau of Indian Affairs to provide various services for Indians enrolled to the Central Council.

An offshoot of the Central Council is the Southeast Alaska Regional Health Consortium - SEARHC, contracts with the federal government to provide public health services in this part of Alaska. In addition to managing the Mount Edgecumbe hospital in Sitka, SEARCH operates a large clinic in Juneau and provides a variety of health and medical services to the small towns and villages of the region.

From the Land Claims Settlement Act to the Present

When Alaska became the 49th State on January 3, 1959, it was allowed to withdraw 102.5 million acres of federal lands along with 400,000 acres of national forest. The purpose of this withdrawal was to allow the new state to become economically independent. As soon as the State began its land selection in the interior, Natives filed a protest, claiming that under the Organic Act of 1884, the State was taking lands which belonged to them. In 1962 the Native newspaper, The Tundra Times, made its debut under the editorship of Howard Rock. He became the spokesman for the Native people, especially regarding human rights and land claims. From across the new State, Indians and Eskimos formed the Alaska Native Federation and demanded payment for the lands taken from them. By 1966, the Natives had filed claims to more than 372 million acres of Alaska.

In the meantime, oil had been discovered in Alaska, and in 1968, an immense oil deposit was located at Prudhoe Bay on the north slope of the Brooks Range. Two years earlier, Secretary of the Interior Stewart Udall had imposed a "land freeze" on all State land selections until a determination could be made concerning Native claims. Conservation groups feared that uncontrolled exploitation of Alaska would destroy the wildlife and wilderness of the "Last Frontier." On the other hand, oil companies wanted to construct a pipeline to transport the oil, but the proposed route crossed lands claimed by the Indians and Eskimos. The State of Alaska also wanted to select lands for its own use. The "land freeze" brought about an unusual coalition. The oil companies and the State came together to push for a settlement with the Natives so that industrial development could continue. A series of bills and proposals were submitted to Congress. The real battle was not simply between Natives and the State or federal government; the underlying dispute

Watercolor by Mark Myers, RSMA,F/ASMA, maritime artist, depicting Tlingit and Haida leaders welcoming Capt. George Vancouver at Port Stewart, near Ketchikan, on Sept. 1, 1793. Based upon extensive historical research. (Original in a private collection, photo by Steve Henrickson)

Reconstruction of a typical Tlingit permanent winter house. This is the "Beaver House" located in the Saxman Totem Park, Saxman, Alaska. (Photo by Wallace Olson)

was between industrial developers such as the oil companies and the conservationists. Native leaders saw it as a rare opportunity to enlist support for their land claims settlement. It was not, as some people described it, a response of the American sense of justice towards the Native people; it was an economic action, pure and simple. The whole outcome of the legislation--and the controversies up to the present time--can only be understood as a battle between the developers and the conservationists.

Since lands outside of the Tongass National Forest had been excluded from consideration in the 1968 settlement, the Central Council of the Tlingit-Haida joined in the land claims on the basis that Natives still had title to nearly two million acres of land.

The final draft of the Act, consisting of 29 pages of tightly-worded text, was rushed through Congress. On December 18, 1971, President Nixon signed into law the Alaska Native Claims Settlement Act.

In return for relinquishing their claims to the lands, the Native people were to receive $962.5 million from the State and Federal governments while retaining title to approximately 40 million acres. But the money and the land were not to go directly to individuals. The Act established 12 regional corporations and more than 200 corporations for traditional Native villages. Today, many Natives question the wisdom of the corporate model for the settlement.

The Settlement Act was extremely complex, with some people calling it the "attorneys' perpetual employment act." The implementation moved slowly. For example, the first step was to have every Native enrolled as a stockholder in a regional and village corporation. It was estimated that enrollment would be completed in a year or two; in fact, it continued for several years. The Natives looked forward to receiving title to their lands in a short time but ten years after the passage of the Act, some corporations still did not have title to their lands. According to the legislation, only those Natives born prior to December 18, 1971, were eligible for enrollment. The plan was for future generations to inherit the shares of stock from those who were corporate shareholders. Some Natives had wanted all Natives in all future generations to receive shares in the corporations.

The Act allocated the money on a per capita basis. The Indians of Southeastern had only given up a small proportion of the land, but since they comprised nearly 20% of the population, they were to get one-fifth of all the money. Eventually, Sealaska, the regional corporation for Southeastern Alaska, received more than $250 million.

The allocation of the 40 million acres of land was also very complicated. Villages were allowed to select their lands basically for subsistence purposes. They were given title to the surface of their lands while their local regional corporation received title to the subsurface rights. Under the Act, only traditional Native villages or settlements with more than 25 Native residents were considered traditional villages. This meant that recent settlements such as Sitka, Ketchikan, Wrangell and Juneau were not considered as "Native villages." As a result, some communities which had a large Native population, were not considered "Native villages" and could not select lands for their people. Later, Juneau and Sitka formed village corporations and now the people registered to this area are shareholders in Goldbelt and Shee Atika Corporations. On the other hand, a large area such as the Stikine kwáan does not have a village corporation to represent it. (See Map page ii and Key to Map page ii)

The regional corporations were allowed to select other lands to which they received both surface and subsurface rights. In Southeastern, since there had been an earlier settlement and the timber was so valuable, the Sealaska Corporation was originally allowed to select only 65,000 acres. Each village corporation in this region was allowed to select one township or 23,040 acres. As the corporations proceeded with their selections, several disputes arose and as a result the allocations were increased. The final compromises gave Sealaska Corporation many thousands of

88

additional acres. Besides the lands allowed for subsistence and commercial development, each corporation was permitted to set aside historic sites and cemeteries. The underlying goal was that with the money and the lands, the corporations would become profitable and lead their shareholders into the mainstream of the American economy. Understanding that it would take time for the corporations to establish themselves, the Act generally gave them tax exempt status for twenty years. At the same time, corporate stock could not be sold or used for collateral; it could only be passed on by inheritance. After twenty years, or in 1991, all shares of stock were to be reissued and shareholders allowed to choose if they wanted to sell their shares or not. In the same year, all corporations would become subject to corporate tax laws.

Before long, there were requests to amend the original bill. The original 1971 Act states that up to 80 million acres of federal lands were to be studied for classification as National Parks, Wildlife Refuges, and Wild and Scenic Rivers. On December 2, 1980, Congress passed the Alaska National Interest Lands Conservation Act setting aside more than 100 million acres of land for conservation. In Southeastern, 5.4 million acres were reserved as wilderness, including nearly all of Admiralty Island. It also prescribed that 450 billion board feet of timber were to be allocated for commercial cutting, with most of the logs going to the mills at Sitka and Ketchikan. In the next few years, Native corporations and private industry greatly expanded their logging operations in the region. The results of the clear cutting can now be seen on mountains, valleys and hillsides across Southeastern.

As the Native leaders looked at the 1991 deadline, it became clear that to survive as viable corporations, further changes had to be made to the Settlement Act. It was no secret that large multinational organizations were looking towards takeovers of these new corporations. Although they had received millions of dollars in direct funding, the natural resources of Sealaska (such as timber, minerals and lands) could be worth billions of dollars. The corporations began to lobby Congress for amendments, and on February 3, 1988, Congress passed Public Law 100-241 making substantial alterations to the original Act of 1971. Basically, what the law did was to allow shareholders a choice regarding stocks and enrollment for those born after 1971 followed by corporate restructuring and registration with the Securities Exchange Commission. Most of these changes were designed to protect the corporations and keep them in the hands of Native people if that is what a majority of their shareholders elected to do. Many other technical provisions were inserted to give the Native people more say over their future.

By 1991 there were offers to buy out Sealaska, but no one really knows what the regional corporation is worth. For instance, who can calculate the value of real estate in the Juneau area where Goldbeld holds the surface rights, but Sealaska the subsurface rights? Huna Totem Corporation has sold much of its timber, but what is the value of any gold or mineral deposits on the surface or the subsurface rights of Sealaska?

There are some who say that the Alaska Claims Settlement Act of 1971 was nothing more than a ploy to eventually take away the lands of Native people. It may look like a settlement, they say, but it is only a way to get legal title away from the Indians and into the hands of private investors. Only time will tell whether it was a good settlement or not.

CONTEMPORARY CULTURE

As with many other people, the Tlingit have dispersed around the world, but most of them still reside in Southeastern Alaska. Some villages are predominately Tlingit, but even in these settlements, there are many non-Natives. Most families have telephones, television sets, cars, boats, freezers, and all the other conveniences of modern life. But in spite of the fact that they have these conveniences, it is difficult to make a living in most villages. In the rural areas, the better-paying jobs such as school teachers, cannery managers, and government agents are oftentimes held by non-Tlingit. The villages of Southeastern Alaska have the same problems that confront other rural Alaskan settlements--little or no economic base, high unemployment, high cost of living and little hope for change in the near future. Across Alaska alcoholism and drug addiction have contributed to an extremely high suicide rate among young people. The systematic degradation of the traditional culture by outside agencies has only recently been turned around so that people are again taking pride in their cultural heritage. The elders hope that this renewed pride may help solve some of the social-psychological problems. But as long as there is no real economic opportunity for village people, the problems will continue.

Commercial fishing has become a highly technical and competitive industry compared to traditional methods. Alaskan Natives must abide by all the laws of the State of Alaska, and so when it comes to commercial fishing, they operate under the same rules as everyone else. In an attempt to maintain the fisheries stocks, voters approved a constitutional amendment in 1972 allowing the State to limit the number of licenses issued for salmon fishing. The limited entry permits were issued on point basis, generally going to those who had fished the longest and had the largest investment in equipment. Many Natives were awarded permits for the various types of fisheries such as trolling, gillnetting and seining. These permits could be sold, and over the years, their value has skyrocketed so that today a seine permit may sell for more than $100,000. Some Natives have sold their permits, and in a few places, hardly any Tlingit now have commercial fishing permits. Natives, like other Alaskan residents, buy sports fishing licenses, and are able to take a few salmon for their household use or "subsistence."

The question of "subsistence" has been hotly debated across the State of Alaska. For thousands of years, Native people, especially those in rural villages, have relied upon their harvest of local plants, fish and land animals for their daily subsistence.

According to the Alaska National Interest Lands Conservation Act (ANILCA) of 1980, if hunting and fishing have to be restricted to protect any species, rural Alaskans will be given preference in hunting and fishing because of their use of these foods for subsistence. However, the constitution of the State of Alaska says that all Alaskans shall have equal access to the resources. The conflict over this issue has polarized the people of the State.

Most of the Indian villages in Southeastern have logged portions of their lands. Generally they have hired outside firms to do the actual logging, and only a small percentage of the local residents make a living in the logging industry. The shareholders do share in the profits which their corporations make through the sale of logs. The problem is that the forests in this northern rain forest are relatively slow-growing, and as the old growth forests are cut, it will take one to two hundred years before they are restored. Some villages, hoping to share in the visitor industry, are beginning to realize that huge tracts of clear-cut forests are not attractive to tourists and they must decide if they want to continue logging or preserve their local environment for tourism.

Many Tlingit have migrated to the small towns and cities of Sitka, Ketchikan and Juneau to find employment in government and private industry. The regional corporation, Sealaska, provides a limited number of jobs for its shareholders, and a few individuals have achieved well-paying, responsible positions. Quite a few Tlingit now live outside of Alaska and so the Sealaska Corporation has held two of its annual meetings in Seattle to accommodate the many shareholders who live there.

The bonds between village and urban people are strengthened through frequent trips back and forth, and by various ceremonies and celebrations. In many ways, the villages tend to be more traditional than the cities, but it is not at all unusual to find people in town coming together for memorials or other services. The Sealaska Heritage Foundation, a non-profit branch of the Sealaska Corporation, has sponsored several "Celebrations" in which elderly people are brought to Juneau for several days of singing, dancing , speeches, and ceremonies.

Because of geographic dispersal, there have been major shifts in the social organization of the Tlingit. The old ways worked well as long as people lived in the same area and shared a common cultural pattern. For the past hundred years, Tlingit have married non-Natives, and this intermarriage has weakened the old kinship system. As newcomers move into the villages, the traditional culture has undergone some major shifts. To a certain extent, the old social order is more influential in the village setting since the population is smaller and the people can continue old customs. While young people from the rural areas oftentimes know their exact clan or lineage, some of their urban counterparts only know that they are Eagle or Raven, but don't really know to which particular clan they belong. At a modern memorial for the dead, people oftentimes participate not by clan but simply on the basis that they are Raven or Eagle.

Several organizations now provide social support in both rural and urban communities. ANB and ANS camps can be found in every village or town, and in large cities like Juneau, there may be more than one camp. They have weekly meetings, sponsor bingo games and other fund raisers, and furnish space for gatherings and memorials. The Tlingit-Haida Central Council provides jobs and scholarships and also acts as a contracting agent for government assistance to the people. For several years, the Sealaska Heritage Foundation funded an applied research program to transcribe stories and speeches to be preserved for future generations. The Sealaska Corporation also has a theater program which takes old legends and transforms them into modern plays. The Naa Ka Hidi Theater has gained recognition and respect from both the Native and non-Native communities. The Sealaska Heritage Foundation continues to provide scholarships for post secondary education and training. In recent years, several village corporations have expanded into the visitor industry.

93

The religious and educational activities which were formerly part of clan and lineage life have now been taken over by the churches and schools. Most Tlingit are members of Christian denominations, and some organizations such as the Salvation Army and the Presbyterian Church have worked with the Native people for many years. Some Tlingit are still active members of the Orthodox Church. There is little, if any, interdenominational competition; it is not at all unusual at a memorial service to see members of the Presbyterian choir join with the Salvation Army, Orthodox Church and others in a sung prayer for the deceased. Some aspects of the old belief system as well as practices and customs still persist. For instance, even though the missionaries tried to eliminate shamanistic practices, a few individuals continue to use them to bring good luck in hunting or fishing.

Language is a key to cultural preservation, but today few people under fifty or sixty years of age are able to speak Tlingit fluently. Even the founders of the ANB realized that to compete in modern society, they needed to speak English. In modern times, there are many Tlingit who are more fluent in computer languages than they are in their traditional tongue. There have been attempts to revive the language, but it appears now that before long, no children will learn to speak the language except for those who study it in school. The race is on, then, to record as much of the traditional oral history, folklore, legends and speeches before the language dies out.

In the past, extensive collections of Tlingit art were purchased or perhaps simply taken for museums in other States and countries. Some of the finest examples of old Tlingit art are no longer in Alaska. Thus, young artists in the villages cannot study the old masterpieces; they have to be content to look at photographs or travel outside of Alaska to see original works. But in spite of these difficulties, Tlingit art has not only been preserved; it has grown in value and importance. Art collectors appreciate the great beauty of Northwest Coast art, and presently it is in great demand. Although the basic forms and designs can still be seen in modern Tlingit art, there have been many changes; it is a living, changing tradition. A few artists are acknowledged masters of design and technique, putting on shows and exhibits around the world. Weavers who learned the skills from their mothers, now teach courses for the school systems and give museum demonstrations. As long as experts like these are available, the art forms will survive. The question right now is whether or not they will continue as an authentic cultural form when so many other aspects of the culture have changed. One of the changes has been that many non-Indian artists have learned the skills of design, color and carving of Northwest Coast art and are producing items for sale. Even though the artistic tradition continues, it is no longer limited to Tlingit people.

CONCLUSION

Looking at contemporary Tlingit culture, one is tempted to ponder the future. Two hundred years ago, only Tlingit shared their culture. Their way of life was integrated so that their subsistence, housing, technology, art, social life, religion, were linked to each other. Today, those components have pulled apart, and with good reason. People no longer want to live in traditional planked clan houses--they prefer central heating and running water. They can no longer send their son off to an uncle who today lives thousands of miles away. Their religious views have changed, and many of the old ways have been forgotten. The Tlingit language is no longer spoken in daily life except by a small number of the elderly.

The future of the culture depends upon the choices of the Tlingit people themselves. They must determine what parts, what aspects, what pieces of their culture they want to preserve for posterity. There is no doubt, though, that Tlingit culture arose out of a time, place, and society along the Northwest Coast and survived for many, many generations. It has a strength and vitality that will keep much of it alive for many more generations to come.

Shopping for Tlingit Art

In recent years there has been a renewed interest in Northwest Coast art including that of the Tlingit, Haida, and Tsimshian Indians of Alaska. In selecting any art the primary consideration must be personal preference--choose those things which appeal to you and that you find attractive. If you decide to purchase an expensive item or make an investment in art, it would be wise to seek the advice of an expert or at least read a few books on Northwest Coast art beforehand. There are many good explanations of the art from this area, but Bill Holm's Northwest Coast Indian Art: An Analysis of Form and Hilary Stewart's Looking at Indian Art of the Northwest Coast are both excellent sources of information for the beginner.

The Tlingit were master woodworkers, and with the advent of metal tools they expanded their art to a variety of materials and forms. Modern artists continue to carve large and small totem poles, hats, masks, rattles, paddles, batons, halibut hooks, bowls, spoons, plaques, and boxes. A few individuals still make bentwood boxes, and occasionally the boxes are carved or painted in traditional designs. In addition to woodcarving, many artists now produce silver or gold bracelets, pins, earrings, and pendants. The truly hand-carved pieces can be quite expensive, depending on the quality of the work and the reputation of the artists. There are cheap, mass-produced replicas such as plastic totem poles or stamped metal bracelets which incorporate Northwest Coast designs; these items should not be confused with the authentic handmade works of art.

Silkscreen prints and posters are other modern art forms that have become popular in recent years. Since silkscreen prints are a new medium, artists are experimenting with many variations from the traditional forms and patterns; entirely new designs are emerging.

There are a few basic qualities in the carvings and paintings that one needs to consider when buying any art beyond mere souvenirs, trinkets, or mementoes. Here are some things to look for:

- The quality of the material used. Is the wood solid, without cracks or gouges? Is the paper a good rag paper, or acid-free, and not creased, torn or finger marked? Is the metal of good quality silver or gold? Many reputable art dealers will provide a certificate of quality for expensive works of art.

- Are the designs well laid out with adequate space and are they fitted well to the shape of the material? Do the formlines flow smoothly from one part to the other? Are the lines crisp and clear with no rough or blurred edges or miscuts? Is there good proportion and balance that reflect traditional Northwest Coast designs? In carvings, are the cuts clean and exact with graceful curves and true straight lines in the cross hatching? Is there attention to detail even in the corners and the edges? In boxes, bowls and masks, are the interior or back areas as equally well carved and finished as the rest of the work?

In addition to the carvings and painted works, the Tlingit and other Northwest Coast Indians were famous for their weaving. The beautiful Chilkat blankets and tunics are now so rare and expensive that anyone who plans to purchase one should first contact an expert for an appraisal. A few women still make button blankets for sale, and they range in quality and price from inexpensive to very expensive, again depending on the quality of the work and the reputation of the artist.

Tlingit and Haida women were famous for their basketry, and there are still some excellent weavers to be found even today. The Tlingit and Haida both used spruce roots for their basketry, while the Haida also used red cedar bark. There are variations in the weaving techniques as well as in designs. In addition to baskets as containers, the Indians made broad brimmed hats from woven root or bark. Baskets will range in price depending on their size and quality. The hats are generally very expensive since it may take a more than a hundred hours to complete a single large hat. In any basketry or weaving, the following are a few qualities to consider:

- Is the material of uniform size and quality so that there are even-sized strips of bark or root? Is the weaving even and consistent with all the ends tucked in and the edges securely finished so it won't unravel? Is the shape or design symmetrical and balanced with an appealing form? If there are attachments such as lids or handles, are they also well-made and carefully fitted to the rest of the article? Finally, do they appear to be sturdy and undamaged?

These are a few simple guidelines for purchasing modern articles. Anyone considering the purchase of antique artifacts will find that they are very expensive and are advised to seek expert assistance and guidance before investing.

RECOMMENDED READINGS

There are many books and articles written about the Tlingit, some of them are very good while others are filled with erroneous data and interpretation. The following list contains suggested readings which are accurate and generally based upon reliable information. Only books which are generally available in most libraries or bookstores are included in this list; those seeking more detailed and scholarly works should seek the assistance of a librarian familiar with Alaskan topics.

GENERAL INFORMATION
Sturdevant, William

1990   Handbook of North American Indians, Volume 7, Northwest Coast. Smithsonian Institution, Washington, D.C. (This book is available in most university libraries.) The volumes in this series each contain articles on each region ranging from archaeology to history and modern issues. The Northwest Coast volume provides a broad background to the entire area with some specific articles on the Tlingit.

GEOLOGY, PREHISTORY AND ENVIRONMENT
Connor, Cathy and Daniel O'Haire

1988   Roadside Geology of Alaska. Mountain Press Publishing Co. Missoula, Montana.
This is an excellent elementary text on Alaska geology with many good photos and illustrations. Pages 18 through 100 deal specifically with Southeastern Alaska. Anyone interested in geology and traveling through the State by car or ferry, will find this a very readable and useful text. *Highly recommended.*

Roppel, Patricia

1978   <u>Southeast: Alaska's Panhandle.</u> Alaska Geographic, Vol. 5, # 2. Edmonds, Washington.

The Alaska Geographic Society has a series of publications on Alaska, and all of them are excellent sources of information with many photos. These publications are very readable and are similar to the National Geographic in format. Other titles in the series are: <u>Admiralty...Island in Contention, The Silver Years of the Alaska Canned Salmon Industry, Glacier Bay; Old Ice, New Land, The Stikine, Sitka and Its Ocean/Island World, Alaska's Salmon Fisheries, Chilkat River Valley</u>.

Stewart, Hilary

1996   *Stone, Bone, Antler & Shell*: Artifacts of the Northwest Coast Indians. University of Washington Press, Seattle.

Although there is no book available on the archaeology of Southeastern Alaska, this publication is a good description of the kinds of artifacts found on the Northwest Coast, including Southeastern Alaska. Archaeologists are slowly compiling the prehistoric record of this region. As new sites are discovered there are oftentimes new explanations so that year by year there are changes in the interpretations. The text, photographs, and illustrations interact to provide a superb picture of the prehistoric tools of this area. *Highly recommended.*

TRADITIONAL CULTURE

Dauenhauer, Richard and Nora

1976   <u>Beginning Tlingit</u>, Tlingit Readers, Inc., Juneau, Alaska.

1984   <u>Tlingit Spelling Book</u>, Sealaska Heritage Foundation Press. Juneau, Alaska.

(An audio cassette can be purchased for use with the Spelling Book.) For many years, the Dauenhauers have researched and published materials on the Tlingit language and translations of speeches and stories. The Sealaska Heritage Foundation sponsors many cultural projects and can provide a current list of materials available to those interested in the language and culture.

Dauenhauer, Nora Marks and Richard, editors.

1987   Haa Shuka, *Our Ancestors*: Tlingit Oral Narratives, Classics of Tlingit Oral Literature Vol.1. University of Washington Press, Seattle Washington, and Sealaska Heritage Foundation, Juneau, Alaska.

1990   *Haa Tuwunaagu Yis*, for Healing Our Spirit: Tlingit Oratory, Classics of Tlingit Oral Literature, Vol.2. University of Washington Press, Seattle, Washington and Sealaska Heritage Foundation, Juneau, Alaska.

These two volumes provide a great deal of information and insight into Tlingit culture and oral literature. The Tlingit texts, in the modern writing system, are presented on the left hand pages, while the English translation appears on the facing right hand page. In addition to the texts, Volume 1 gives an extended explanation of Tlingit oratory and the written language. Volume 2, devotes the first one hundred and fifty pages to an explanation of Tlingit society and the memorial for the dead. The remaining four hundred pages again show the texts in both languages. At the end, there is a glossary and several short biographies of Tlingit elders.

101

1994   *Haa Kusteeyí* Our Culture: Tlingit Life Stories, Classics of Tlingit Oral Literature, Vol. 3, University of Washington Press, Seattle, Washington, and Sealaska Heritage Foundation, Juneau. These 53 biographies of Tlingit leaders describe the challenges and accomplishments of individuals who shaped the history of their people. The 121 page introduction summarizes tradtional Tlingit social structure along with historical changes and adaptations. This third volume in the award-winning series on Tlingit cultural heritage, with its historical photographs, gives the reader a deeper insight into the lives of individual Tlingits and their place in Alaskan history.

DeLaguna, Frederica

1972   Under Mount St. Elias; The History and Culture of the Yakutat Tlingit. (3 volumes)
Smithsonian Institution, Washington, D.C.
This is the most thorough study of the Tlingit ever published. The author is considered one of the foremost authorities on the Tlingit and has written many other books and articles about them. Nearly all of her books are government publications or articles in scholarly journals but are available in most large libraries.

Drucker, Philip

1965   Cultures of the North Pacific Coast.
Chandler Publishing Co., San Francisco, California.
An excellent introduction to the cultures of this area. Drucker has several other publications all of which are very informative and well written.

Emmons, George Thornton

1991   The Tlingit Indians. Edited with additions by Frederica de Laguna and biography by Jean Low. University of Washington Press. Emmons was in Southeastern Alaska in the 1880s and 1890s as a Navy Lieutenant. He spent a great deal of time with Tlingit, and later collected and purchased many artifacts for museums across the country. He became famous for many articles on Tlingit culture, with extensive photos and illustrations. He never completed a definitive work on the Tlingit, so Dr. DeLaguna organized his notes and manuscripts for publication. This is the latest, and one of the finest books about the Tlingit.

The Tlingit Indians and Under Mount St. Elias are the two best descriptions of the Tlingit, their culture and history.

Jonaitis, Aldona

1986   Art of the Northern Tlingit.

University of Washington Press, Seattle, Washington.

A rather specialized study on Tlingit art based on a contrast between sacred and social art but does give a general description of Tlingit art. There are many art catalogs and publications showing Tlingit art, but this is one of the few books that attempt to describe its cultural setting.

Kan, Sergei

1989   Symbolic Immortality: The Tlingit Potlatch of the Nineteenth Century. Smithsonian Institution Press, Washington, D.C.

This is a scholarly, interpretive study of the Tlingit memorial services, the person and social order and values. The book provides insights into the psychology, philosophy and religion of the people.

Krause, Aurel
  1885   The Tlingit Indians.
             Translated from the German by Erna Gunther in 1956.
             University of Washington Press, Seattle, Washington.
             A description of the Tlingit in the 1880's, limited in
             scope but still a good introduction.

Naish, Constance and Gillian Story
  1976   English-Tlingit Dictionary, Nouns, Sheldon Jackson
             College, Sitka, Alaska.
             This is a dictionary of some English words translated
             into Tlingit. It is intended for the average person
             without special training. The Alaska Native Language
             Center at the University of Alaska Fairbanks, has
             additional dictionaries and texts for studying the
             Tlingit language.

Oberg, Kalvero
  1973   The Social Economy of the Tlingit Indians. University
             of Washington Press, Seattle, Washington.
             This is a classic study of Tlingit economy based upon
             field work in Klukwan, Alaska in the 1930's.

Olson, Marie (Kaayistaan)
  1995   A Tlingit Coloring Book Heritage Research, Auke
             Bay, Alaska. The author's Tlingit name is Kaayistaan.
             This is a 24-page book, 8 ½ by 11 inches, with line
             drawings of objects and resources from traditional
             Tlingit culture along with the Tlingit names for the
             objects. It has a color-by-number system and includes

the names for the fingers and how to count to ten in Tlingit.

Stewart, Hilary

1977   Indian Fishing: Early Methods on the Northwest Coast. University of Washington Press, Seattle, Washington.

As with her other writings, Hilary Stewart's text looks at the entire Northwest Coast for a comparative study of fishing techniques and technology. In addition to the fishing techniques, she also explains and illustrates the methods of cooking fish. The final portion gives a brief insight into the spiritual significance of fish and fishing for the people of the Northwest Coast.

1979   Looking at Indian Art of the Northwest Coast. University of Washington Press, Seattle, Washington.

The author, a skilled artist in her own right, examines the various components, features and motifs of Northwest Coast art, using both text and illustrations. Although a small book (110 pages), it is an excellent guide for the analysis of this classical art form.

1984   Cedar: Tree of Life to the Northwest Coast Indians. University of Washington Press, Seattle, Washington.

As the title indicates, the cedar was the choice material for houses, canoes, boxes, weaving, clothing and a host of other Northwest Coast artifacts. Stewart discusses cedar from its botanical aspects to its spiritual value to the people. The exquisite illustrations are balanced by a very clear and complete text. The book is useful not just for its information on the cedar, but even more for its insights into Native life on the Northwest Coast.

Swanton, John

1909   Tlingit Myths and Texts.
        U.S.Bureau of Ethnology, Bulletin 39, Washington,
        D.C.
        Swanton worked in Southeastern Alaska in the early
        1900's and published many works which are
        considered the pioneering studies of the region. His
        other study, Social Conditions, Beliefs and Linguistic
        Relationship of the Tlingit Indians, is a small book but
        contains a great deal of information.

HISTORICAL CHANGES

Arnold, Robert D.

1976   Alaska Native Land Claims. Alaska Native
        Foundation, Anchorage, Alaska.
        Although there have been many changes to the original
        land claims settlement act since 1976 when this book
        was first published, this is still a basic reference for
        the history of the claims movement. It explains the
        original provisions and illustrates them through the
        use of charts and maps.

Chevigny, Hector

1965   Russian America: The Great Alaska Adventure, 1741-
        1867. Viking Press, New York.
        A good introduction to the history of Russian
        America. The author has two other biographies
        entitled Lord of Alaska (Alexander Baranov) and Lost
        Empire (Nicolai Resanov). Many authorities consider
        Chevigny's works to be "historical fiction" rather than
        precise information and interpretation. The Limestone
        Press, P.O. Box 1604, Kingston, Ontario, Canada
        K7L 5C8, has published translations of many other
        Russian accounts of Russian America.

Menzies, Archibald

1994   *The Alaska Travel Journal of Archibald Menzies, 1793-94.* (With an introduction and annotation by Wallace Olson and list of botanical collections by John F. Thilenius.) Fairbanks, University of Alaska Press.

Menzies was the botanist-naturalist with Vancouver and kept his own diary. This publication covers the period when he was in Southeastern Alaska and contains some descriptions of the Tlingit.

Naske, Claus and Herman Slotnick

1987   Alaska: A History of the 49th State. 2nd Edition, University of Oklahoma Press, Norman, Oklahoma.

This is the latest general textbook of Alaskan history. It includes basic information regarding the Native people and their relationship to the other events from the days of Russian colonization through Statehood and the discovery of oil.

Tikhmenev, P.A.

1978   A History of the Russian-American Company. Translated by R.A. Pierce and A. Donnelly, University of Washington Press, Seattle, Washington.

The original Russian text was published in the early 1860's to glorify the works of the Company. A good description of activities during this time from the Company's point of view.

VIDEO CASSETTES

1988   *KEET SHAGOON*:The origin of the killer whale. (28 minutes) VHS 1/2"

1990   The Box of Daylight: A Tlingit Myth of Creation. (81/2 minutes) VHS 1/2"

These two cassettes have been produced by Naa Kahidi Theater, a program of the Sealaska Heritage Foundation, One Sealaska Plaza, Juneau, Alaska 99801. They can be found in gift stores, or may be ordered directly from the Sealaska Heritage Foundation.

The productions are modern theater adaptations of traditional Tlingit stories and are performed by Tlingit actors in pre-European costumes and regalia. School children and adults will find these to be entertaining and instructive. In the future, Naa Kahidi Theater hopes to video record other performances.

1996   Seeing Daylight: Alaska's Tlingit and their Culture (30 minutes) VHS 1/2"

A docu-drama, describing aspects of the traditional culture and historic changes, produced by Mount Roberts Tramway Limited Partnership and available at the Mount Roberts Tramway or through Goldbelt Corporation. Some aspects of the old culturee are portrayed by Tlingit in traditional dress. The final portion describes the influence of the Goldbelt Corporation in modern life.